みんなの日本語 初級I 第2版

Minna no Nihongo

Romanized Version

Elementary Japanese I Second Edition
Translation & Grammar Notes—English

翻訳・文法解説
ローマ字版【英語】

スリーエーネットワーク

© 2000 by 3A Corporation

All rights reserved. No part of this publication may be reproduced, stored in a retrieval system or transmitted in any form or by any means, electronic, mechanical, photocopying, recording, or otherwise, without the prior written permission of the Publisher.

Published by 3A Corporation.
Trusty Kojimachi Bldg., 2F, 4, Kojimachi 3-Chome, Chiyoda-ku, Tokyo 102-0083, Japan

ISBN978-4-88319-629-6 C0081

First published 2000
Second Edition 2013
Printed in Japan

FOREWORD

As the title *Minna no Nihongo* indicates, this book has been designed to make the study of Japanese as enjoyable and interesting as possible for students and teachers alike. Over three years in the planning and compilation, it stands as a complete textbook in itself while acting as a companion volume to the highly-regarded *Shin Nihongo no Kiso*.

As readers may know, *Shin Nihongo no Kiso* is a comprehensive introduction to elementary Japanese that serves as a highly efficient resource enabling students wishing to master basic Japanese conversation to do so in the shortest possible time. As such, although it was originally developed for use by AOTS's technical trainees, it is now used by a wide range of people both in Japan and abroad.

The teaching of Japanese is branching out in many different ways. Japanese economic and industrial growth has led to a greater level of interchange between Japan and other countries, and non-Japanese from a wide variety of backgrounds have come to Japan with a range of different objectives and are now living within local communities here. The changes in the social milieu surrounding the teaching of Japanese that have resulted from this influx of people from other countries have in turn influenced the individual situations in which Japanese is taught. There is now a greater diversity of learning needs, and they require individual responses.

It is against this background, and in response to the opinions and hopes expressed by a large number of people who have been involved in the teaching of Japanese for many years both in Japan and elsewhere, that 3A Corporation proudly publishes *Minna no Nihongo*. While the book continues to make use of the clarity and ease of understanding provided by the special features, key learning points and learning methods of *Shin Nihongo no Kiso*, the scenes, situations and characters in *Minna no Nihongo* have been made more universal in order to appeal to a wider range of learners. Its contents have been enhanced in this way to allow all kinds of students to use it for studying Japanese with pleasure.

Minna no Nihongo is aimed at anyone who urgently needs to learn to communicate in Japanese in any situation, whether at work, school, college or in their local community. Although it is an introductory text, efforts have been made to make the exchanges between Japanese and foreign characters in the book reflect Japanese social conditions and everyday life as faithfully as possible. While it is intended principally for those who have already left full-time education, it can also be recommended as an excellent textbook for university entrance courses as well as for short-term intensive courses at technical colleges and universities.

We at 3A Corporation are continuing actively to produce new study materials designed to meet the individual needs of an increasingly wide range of learners, and we sincerely hope that readers will continue to give us their valued support.

In conclusion, I should like to mention the extensive help we received in the preparation of this text, in the form of suggestions and comments from various quarters, and trials of the materials in actual lessons, for which we are extremely grateful. 3A Corporation intends to continue extending its network of friendship all over the world through activities such as the publishing of Japanese study materials, and we hope that everyone who knows us will continue to lend us their unstinting encouragement and support in this.

Iwao Ogawa
President, 3A Corporation
March 1998

FOREWORD TO THE SECOND EDITION

— On the Publication of the Second Edition of *Minna no Nihongo Shokyu* —

We are proud to publish the second edition of **Minna no Nihongo Shokyu**. As stated in the Foreword to the first edition, **Minna no Nihongo Shokyu** can be regarded as a companion volume to **Shin Nihongo no Kiso**, a textbook originally developed for technical trainees.

The first printing of the first edition of **Minna no Nihongo Shokyu I** was issued in March 1998, when great changes in the social environment surrounding the teaching of Japanese were taking place. The burgeoning of relationships between Japan and the rest of the world had led to a rapid increase in the number of students of Japanese and their reasons for studying the language, and the consequent diversification of their requirements had necessitated a response more tailored to learners' individual situations. 3A Corporation published **Minna no Nihongo Shokyu** in response to suggestions and comments received from people on the front lines of Japanese teaching in Japan and elsewhere.

Minna no Nihongo Shokyu was acclaimed for its easily-understood key learning points and methods, its high degree of general applicability that took into account learners' diversity, and for being a carefully-crafted learning resource that was outstandingly effective for students attempting to master Japanese conversation quickly. It has served well for over ten years, but any language changes with the times, and both Japan and other countries have experienced great upheavals recently. Particularly in the last few years, the environment in which the Japanese language and its learners are situated has changed drastically.

In these circumstances, 3A Corporation decided to review and partially revise **Minna no Nihongo Shokyu I** and **II**, based on our publishing and training experience and reflecting the many opinions and questions we have received from students and teachers of Japanese, in order to be able to contribute further to the teaching of Japanese as a foreign language.

The revision focused on making the book even more usable and changing any words or scenarios that no longer reflected current conditions. Respecting the wishes of students and teachers, we have preserved the original textbook format, which has the benefit of making the book easy to use for both learning and teaching, and we have introduced more exercises and practice questions designed to strengthen students' active language ability by inviting them to understand situations for themselves and think about how to express themselves, rather than merely following instructions and practising in a passive way. We have included a large number of illustrations for this purpose.

We are extremely grateful for the enormous help we received in the editing of this book, in the form of comments and suggestions from various quarters, and trials in actual lessons. 3A Corporation intends to continue developing textbooks that can not only help students of Japanese to communicate what they need to but also contribute to international interpersonal interchange, and we hope that everyone engaged in such activities will find them useful. We warmly invite everyone who knows us to continue to lend us their unstinting encouragement and support in this.

Takuji Kobayashi
President, 3A Corporation
June 2012

TO USERS OF THIS BOOK

Ⅰ. Structure

The second edition of *Minna no Nihongo Shokyu I* consists of two volumes: the Main Text (with CD) and the Translation and Grammar Notes. We plan to publish the Translation and Grammar Notes in twelve languages, starting with English.

The materials have been compiled with the aim of inculcating the four skills of speaking, listening, reading and writing. However the Main Text and the Translation and Grammar Notes do not provide any instruction in reading and writing hiragana, katakana, or kanji.

Ⅱ. Contents

1. Main Text

1) Japanese Pronunciation

This section gives examples of the chief points to note concerning Japanese pronunciation.

2) Classroom Language, Everyday Greetings and Expressions, Numerals

This section contains a list of words and phrases used in the classroom, basic everyday greetings, and so on.

3) Lessons

There are 25 lessons, each containing the following:

① Sentence patterns

Basic sentence patterns to be learned in that lesson.

② Example sentences

Basic sentence patterns incorporated into short dialogues to show how they are used in actual conversation. New adverbs, conjunctions, and other parts of speech, plus further learning points, are also introduced.

③ Conversation

In the conversation, foreign people living in Japan appear in a variety of situations. The conversation includes everyday greetings and other expressions and as well as the material to be learned in the lesson. If time allows, students can try developing the conversation by introducing some of the Useful Words given in the Translation and Grammar Notes.

④ Exercises

The exercises are split into three levels: A, B, and C.

Exercise A is laid out visually to help students understand the grammatical structure easily. It has been designed to make it easy for students to practise conjugating verbs and forming connections, as well as mastering the basic sentence patterns.

Exercise B employs various forms to strengthen students' grasp of the basic sentence patterns. A number with an arrow (➡) indicates an exercise that uses an illustration.

Exercise C is designed to help students improve their communication abilities. Students use this exercise to practise conversing while substituting the underlined words in the designated conversation with alternatives matching the situation; however, to prevent this becoming a simple substitution drill, we have wherever possible avoided using words to indicate substitutions. This means that the exercises are very free, with students able to create various different conversational examples based on a single illustration.

Model answers to Exercises B and C are available in a separate compilation volume.

⑤ Practice questions

There are three types of practice question: listening comprehension, grammar, and reading comprehension. The listening comprehension questions are further subdivided into two types: answering short questions, and listening to short conversations and grasping the key points. The grammar questions check students' understanding of vocabulary and grammar points. For the reading comprehension questions, students read a simple passage incorporating vocabulary and grammar they have already studied, and perform various types of task relating to its contents.

⑥ Review

This is provided to enable students to go over the essential points once more every few lessons.

⑦ Summary of Adverbs, Conjunctions and Conversational Expressions

These are practice questions designed to enable students to review the adverbs, conjunctions and conversational expressions presented in this textbook.

4) Verb forms

This section summarises the verb forms presented in this textbook, together with various forms added to the ends of verbs.

5) Table of Key Learning Points

This is a summary of the key learning points presented in this textbook, focusing on Exercise A. It indicates which of the Sentence Patterns, Example Sentences, and Exercises B and C are relevant to each of the learning points introduced in Exercise A.

6) **Index**

This includes Classroom Language, Everyday Greetings and Expressions, and new vocabulary and expressions appearing in each lesson, with references to the lesson in which they first appear.

7) **Included CD**

The CD that goes with this book contains the conversation and the listening comprehension exercises from each lesson.

2. Translation and Grammar notes

1) Explanations of the general features of Japanese, as well as the Japanese writing and pronunciation systems.

2) Translations of Classroom Language, and Everyday Greetings and Expressions.

3) The following for each of Lessons 1 through 25:
   ① New words and their translations.
   ② Translations of Sentence Patterns, Example Sentences and Conversations.
   ③ Useful words relevant to each lesson and snippets of information on Japan.
   ④ Explanations of the grammar of the Sentence Patterns and expressions.

4) A summary of how to express numbers, time, and time periods, a list of counter suffixes, and conjugations of verbs.

III. Time Required to Complete the Lessons

As a guideline, it should take students 4-6 hours to cover each lesson, and 150 hours to finish the entire book.

IV. Vocabulary

The book presents approximately 1,000 words, mainly ones used frequently in daily life.

V. Romanization

1) In general, the Hepburn system of romanization has been used.
   The syllabic nasal sound is represented by 'n' throughout.

2) Long vowels are indicated as follows:
   ā, ii, ū, ei (ē), ō
   e.g. okāsan (mother)   ōkii (big, large)   tokei (watch, clock)
   onēsan (elder sister)

3) For readability, the text has been transliterated with spaces between words.
   Particles are written separately except when accepted as forming a single unit with the parent word.
   e.g. nanika (something)   desukara (therefore, so)

4) Prefixes, suffixes and counters are usually separated from their parent words by hyphens, and long compound words are broken up by hyphens.

    e.g. o-shigoto (work, business)   Tanaka-san (Mr. Tanaka)

        25-sai (25 years old)   hana-ya (florist)   benkyō-shimasu (study)

However, the hyphen is omitted when the compound is regarded as a single unit.

    e.g. hitotsu (one)   hitori (one person)   ocha (tea)   asagohan (breakfast)

        oyasuminasai (good night)

5) Capitals are used at the beginning of sentences and for the initial letters of proper nouns.

6) Foreign names are spelt according to the katakana spelling.

    e.g. Mirā-san (Mr. Miller)

7) Some foreign loan words are romanized to approximate their original pronunciation.

    e.g. pātii (party)   fōku (fork)

VI. Miscellaneous

1) Words that can be omitted are enclosed in square brackets:

    e.g. Chichi wa 54 [-sai] desu.   (My father is 54 [years old]).

2) Synonymous words and expressions are enclosed in round brackets:

    e.g. dare (donata)   (who)

HOW TO USE THIS BOOK EFFECTIVELY

1. Learn the words

The Translation and Grammar Notes introduces the new words for each lesson. Learn these new words by practising making short sentences with them.

2. Practise the Sentence Patterns

Make sure you understand the meaning of each sentence pattern, and do Exercises A and B aloud until the pattern becomes automatic.

3. Practise holding conversations

Practise the sentence patterns using the short dialogues given in Exercise C, but don't stop there; carry on and extend the conversations. The conversations simulate everyday situations that students are likely to encounter, and the best way of acquiring a natural conversational rhythm is to act out the conversations using gestures and facial expressions while listening to the CD.

4. Check your understanding

Each lesson ends with some practice questions which you should use to check that you have correctly understood the lesson.

5. Apply what you have learnt

Try talking to Japanese people using the Japanese you have learnt. Applying what you have learnt right away, before you forget it, is the quickest way to progress.

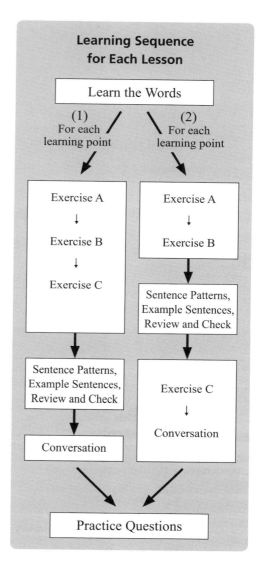

Learning Sequence for Each Lesson

Study the material by following either Route (1) or Route (2). To make sure you cover all the key learning points, please check the Table of Key Learning Points at the end of this book.

CHARACTERS

Mike Miller

American, employee of IMC

Sato Keiko

Japanese, employee of IMC

Jose Santos

Brazilian, employee of Brazil Air

Maria Santos

Brazilian, housewife

Karina

Indonesian, student at Fuji University

Wang Xue

Chinese, doctor at Kobe Hospital

Yamada Ichiro

Japanese, employee of IMC

Yamada Tomoko

Japanese, bank clerk

Matsumoto Tadashi
Japanese,
department chief at IMC

Matsumoto Yoshiko
Japanese, housewife

Kimura Izumi
Japanese, announcer

John Watt
British,
professor at Sakura University

Karl Schmidt
German,
engineer at Power Electric Company

Lee Jin Ju
Korean,
research worker at AKC

Teresa Santos
Brazilian, schoolgirl (9 yrs.),
daughter of Jose and Maria Santos

Yamada Taro
Japanese, schoolboy (8 yrs.),
son of Ichiro and Tomoko Yamada

Gupta
Indian, employee of IMC

Thawaphon
Thai,
student at Japanese language school

※ IMC (computer software company)
※ AKC (Ajia-kenkyū-sentā：Asia Research Institute)

CONTENTS

GENERAL FEATURES OF JAPANESE ·································· 2

JAPANESE WRITING ··································· 2

INTRODUCTION
Ⅰ. Japanese Pronunciation ··································· 3
Ⅱ. Classroom Language ··································· 7
Ⅲ. Everyday Greetings and Expressions ··································· 7

TERMS USED FOR INSTRUCTION ··································· 8
KEY TO SYMBOLS AND ABBREVIATIONS ··································· 9

Lesson 1 ··································· 10

Ⅰ. Vocabulary

Ⅱ. Translation
Sentence Patterns and Example Sentences
Conversation: **How do you do?**

Ⅲ. Useful Words and Information
Countries, People and Languages

Ⅳ. Grammar Notes
1. N_1 wa N_2 desu
2. N_1 wa N_2 ja (dewa) arimasen
3. N_1 wa N_2 desu ka
4. N mo
5. N_1 no N_2
6. -san

Lesson 2 ··································· 16

Ⅰ. Vocabulary

Ⅱ. Translation
Sentence Patterns and Example Sentences
Conversation:
Thank you in advance for your kindness

Ⅲ. Useful Words and Information
Family Names

Ⅳ. Grammar Notes
1. kore/sore/are
2. kono N/sono N/ano N
3. sō desu
4. ～ ka, ～ ka
5. N_1 no N_2
6. no substituting for a noun
7. o-
8. sō desu ka

Lesson 3 ·· 22

I . **Vocabulary**

II . **Translation**

    Sentence Patterns and Example Sentences

    Conversation: **I'll take it, please**

III . **Useful Words and Information**

    Department Store

IV . **Grammar Notes**

    1. koko/soko/asoko/kochira/sochira/ achira

    2. N wa place desu

    3. doko/dochira

    4. N₁ no N₂

    5. The ko/so/a/do system of demonstratives

    6. o-

Lesson 4 ·· 28

I . **Vocabulary**

II . **Translation**

    Sentence Patterns and Example Sentences

    Conversation:

    What time are you open to?

III . **Useful Words and Information**

    Telephone and Letters

IV . **Grammar Notes**

    1. Ima -ji -fun desu

    2. V-masu/V-masen/V-mashita/ V-masendeshita

    3. N (time) ni V

    4. N₁ kara N₂ made

    5. N₁ to N₂

    6. ～ ne

Lesson 5 ·· 34

I . **Vocabulary**

II . **Translation**

    Sentence Patterns and Example Sentences

    Conversation:

    Does this train go to Koshien?

III . **Useful Words and Information**

    National Holidays

IV . **Grammar Notes**

    1. N (place) e ikimasu/kimasu/ kaerimasu

    2. Doko [e] mo ikimasen/ ikimasendeshita

    3. N (vehicle) de ikimasu/kimasu/ kaerimasu

    4. N (person/animal) to V

    5. itsu

    6. ～ yo

    7. sō desu ne

Lesson 6 ·· 40

Ⅰ. Vocabulary
Ⅱ. Translation
    Sentence Patterns and Example Sentences
    Conversation:
      Shall we go together?
Ⅲ. Useful Words and Information
    Food

Ⅳ. Grammar Notes
  1. N o V (transitive)
  2. N o shimasu
  3. Nani o shimasu ka
  4. nan and nani
  5. N (place) de V
  6. V-masen ka
  7. V-mashō
  8. ～ ka

Lesson 7 ·· 46

Ⅰ. Vocabulary
Ⅱ. Translation
    Sentence Patterns and Example Sentences
    Conversation: **Welcome**
Ⅲ. Useful Words and Information
    Family

Ⅳ. Grammar Notes
  1. N (tool/means) de V
  2. 'Word/Sentence' wa -go de
     nan desu ka
  3. N_1 (person) ni N_2 o agemasu, etc.
  4. N_1 (person) ni N_2 o moraimasu, etc.
  5. Mō V-mashita
  6. Omission of particles

Lesson 8 ·· 52

Ⅰ. Vocabulary
Ⅱ. Translation
    Sentence Patterns and Example Sentences
    Conversation:
      It's time we were going
Ⅲ. Useful Words and Information
    Colours and Tastes

Ⅳ. Grammar Notes
  1. Adjectives
  2. N wa na-adj [na] desu
     N wa i-adj (～i) desu
  3. na-adj na N
     i-adj (～i) N
  4. ～ ga, ～
  5. totemo/amari
  6. N wa dō desu ka
  7. N_1 wa donna N_2 desu ka
  8. sō desu ne

Lesson 9 58

Ⅰ. Vocabulary
Ⅱ. Translation
Sentence Patterns and Example Sentences
Conversation: **It's a pity......**
Ⅲ. Useful Words and Information
Music, Sports and Films

Ⅳ. Grammar Notes
1. N ga arimasu/wakarimasu
N ga suki desu/kirai desu/
jōzu desu/heta desu
2. donna N
3. yoku/daitai/takusan/sukoshi/
amari/zenzen
4. ～ kara, ～
5. dōshite

Lesson 10 64

Ⅰ. Vocabulary
Ⅱ. Translation
Sentence Patterns and Example Sentences
Conversation:
Do you have any nam pla?
Ⅲ. Useful Words and Information
Inside the House

Ⅳ. Grammar Notes
1. N ga arimasu/imasu
2. Place ni N ga arimasu/imasu
3. N wa place ni arimasu/imasu
4. N$_1$ (thing/person/place) no N$_2$ (position)
5. N$_1$ ya N$_2$
6. Ajia-sutoa desu ka

Lesson 11 70

Ⅰ. Vocabulary
Ⅱ. Translation
Sentence Patterns and Example Sentences
Conversation:
[I'd like to send] this, please
Ⅲ. Useful Words and Information
Menu

Ⅳ. Grammar Notes
1. How to say numbers
2. How to use quantifiers
3. Quantifier (time period) ni -kai V
4. Quantifier dake/N dake

Lesson 12 76

Ⅰ. Vocabulary
Ⅱ. Translation
Sentence Patterns and Example Sentences
Conversation:
How was the Gion Festival?
Ⅲ. Useful Words and Information
Festivals and Places of Note

Ⅳ. Grammar Notes
1. Tense and affirmative/negative
forms of noun sentences and
na-adjective sentences
2. Tense and affirmative/negative
forms of i-adjective sentences
3. N$_1$ wa N$_2$ yori adj desu
4. N$_1$ to N$_2$ to dochira ga adj desu ka
······N$_1$/N$_2$ no hō ga adj desu
5. N$_1$ [no naka] de nani/doko/dare/itsu
ga ichiban adj desu ka
······N$_2$ ga ichiban adj desu
6. Adj no (no substituting for a noun)

Lesson 13 82

Ⅰ. Vocabulary
Ⅱ. Translation
   Sentence Patterns and Example Sentences
   Conversation: **Separately, please**
Ⅲ. Useful Words and Information
   Town

Ⅳ. **Grammar Notes**
   1. N ga hoshii desu
   2. V masu-form tai desu
   3. N (place) e $\left\{ \begin{array}{l} \text{V masu-form} \\ \text{N} \end{array} \right\}$ ni
      ikimasu/kimasu/kaerimasu
   4. dokoka/nanika
   5. go-

Lesson 14 88

Ⅰ. Vocabulary
Ⅱ. Translation
   Sentence Patterns and Example Sentences
   Conversation: **To Midoricho, please**
Ⅲ. Useful Words and Information
   Station

Ⅳ. **Grammar Notes**
   1. Verb Groups
   2. V te-form
   3. V te-form kudasai
   4. V te-form imasu
   5. V masu-form mashō ka
   6. N ga V
   7. sumimasen ga

Lesson 15 94

Ⅰ. Vocabulary
Ⅱ. Translation
   Sentence Patterns and Example Sentences
   Conversation:
      What family do you have?
Ⅲ. Useful Words and Information
   Occupations

Ⅳ. **Grammar Notes**
   1. V te-form mo ii desu ka
   2. V te-form wa ikemasen
   3. V te-form imasu
   4. N ni V
   5. N_1 ni N_2 o V

Lesson 16 100

Ⅰ. Vocabulary
Ⅱ. Translation
   Sentence Patterns and Example Sentences
   Conversation:
      Please show me how to use it
Ⅲ. Useful Words and Information
   How to Use a Cash Machine

Ⅳ. **Grammar Notes**
   1. How to join two or more sentences
      together
   2. V_1 te-form kara, V_2
   3. N_1 wa N_2 ga adj
   4. N o V
   5. dōyatte
   6. dore/dono N

Lesson 17 ⋯⋯⋯⋯⋯⋯⋯⋯⋯⋯⋯⋯⋯⋯⋯⋯⋯ 106

Ⅰ. Vocabulary

Ⅱ. Translation

　Sentence Patterns and Example Sentences

　Conversation:

　　What seems to be the matter?

Ⅲ. Useful Words and Information

　Body and Illness

Ⅳ. Grammar Notes

　1. V nai-form

　2. V nai-form nai de kudasai

　3. V nai-form nakereba narimasen

　4. V nai-form nakute mo ii desu

　5. Making an object the topic of a sentence

　6. N (time) made ni V

Lesson 18 ⋯⋯⋯⋯⋯⋯⋯⋯⋯⋯⋯⋯⋯⋯⋯⋯⋯ 112

Ⅰ. Vocabulary

Ⅱ. Translation

　Sentence Patterns and Example Sentences

　Conversation:

　　What do you like doing?

Ⅲ. Useful Words and Information

　Actions

Ⅳ. Grammar Notes

　1. Dictionary form of verbs

　2. N / V-dictionary form koto } ga dekimasu

　3. Watashi no shumi wa { N / V-dictionary form koto } desu

　4. V₁-dictionary form / N no / Quantifier (time period) } mae ni, V₂

　5. nakanaka

　6. zehi

Lesson 19 ⋯⋯⋯⋯⋯⋯⋯⋯⋯⋯⋯⋯⋯⋯⋯⋯⋯ 118

Ⅰ. Vocabulary

Ⅱ. Translation

　Sentence Patterns and Example Sentences

　Conversation:

　　I'll start dieting tomorrow

Ⅲ. Useful Words and Information

　Traditional Culture and Entertainment

Ⅳ. Grammar Notes

　1. V ta-form

　2. V ta-form koto ga arimasu

　3. V₁ ta-form ri, V₂ ta-form ri shimasu

　4. i-adj (~い) → ~ku / na-adj [な] → ~ni / N ni } narimasu

Lesson 20 ⋯⋯⋯⋯⋯⋯⋯⋯⋯⋯⋯⋯⋯⋯⋯⋯⋯ 124

Ⅰ. Vocabulary

Ⅱ. Translation

　Sentence Patterns and Example Sentences

　Conversation: **Shall we go together?**

Ⅲ. Useful Words and Information

　How to Address People

Ⅳ. Grammar Notes

　1. Polite style and plain style

　2. Proper use of the polite style or plain style

　3. Conversation in the plain style

Lesson 21 ·· 130

Ⅰ. Vocabulary
Ⅱ. Translation
    Sentence Patterns and Example Sentences
    Conversation: **I think so, too**
Ⅲ. Useful Words and Information
    Positions in Society

Ⅳ. Grammar Notes
  1. Plain form to omoimasu
  2. "Sentences" / Plain form } to iimasu
  3. V } plain form
    i-adj
    na-adj } plain form } deshō?
    N } ~ dá
  4. N₁ (place) de N₂ ga arimasu
  5. N (occasion) de
  6. N demo V
  7. V nai-form nai to······

Lesson 22 ·· 136

Ⅰ. Vocabulary
Ⅱ. Translation
    Sentence Patterns and Example Sentences
    Conversation:
    What kind of flat are you looking for?
Ⅲ. Useful Words and Information
    Clothes

Ⅳ. Grammar Notes
  1. Noun modification
  2. V-dictionary form jikan/yakusoku/yōji
  3. V masu-form mashō ka

Lesson 23 ·· 142

Ⅰ. Vocabulary
Ⅱ. Translation
    Sentence Patterns and Example Sentences
    Conversation:
    How do you get there?
Ⅲ. Useful Words and Information
    Roads and Traffic

Ⅳ. Grammar Notes
  1. V-dictionary form / V nai-form nai / i-adj (~i) / na-adj na / N no } toki, ~ (main clause)
  2. V-dictionary form / V ta-form } toki, ~ (main clause)
  3. V-dictionary form to, ~ (main clause)
  4. N ga adj
  5. N o motionV

Lesson 24

············· 148

I. **Vocabulary**

II. **Translation**

    Sentence Patterns and Example Sentences

    Conversation:

      Shall I come and help?

III. **Useful Words and Information**

      Exchanging Gifts

IV. **Grammar Notes**

    1. kuremasu

    2. V te-form $\begin{cases} \text{agemasu} \\ \text{moraimasu} \\ \text{kuremasu} \end{cases}$

    3. N_1 wa N_2 ga V

Lesson 25

············· 154

I. **Vocabulary**

II. **Translation**

    Sentence Patterns and Example Sentences

    Conversation:

      Thanks for everything

III. **Useful Words and Information**

      Life

IV. **Grammar Notes**

    1. Plain past form ra, ～ (main clause)

    2. V ta-form ra, ～ (main clause)

    3. V te-form

      V nai-form nakute

      i-adj (～ィ)→～kute $\Big\}$ mo, ～ (main clause)

      na-adj [ナ]→～de

      N de

    4. moshi

    5. Subject of a subordinate clause

Article 1 : Topic and Subject ················· 160

Article 2 : Clauses ················· 163

APPENDICES

I. **Numerals** ················· 164

II. **Expressions of time** ················· 165

III. **Expressions of period** ················· 167

IV. **Counter suffixes** ················· 168

V. **Conjugations of verbs** ················· 170

GENERAL FEATURES OF JAPANESE

1. Parts of Speech The Japanese language is composed of verbs, adjectives, nouns, adverbs, conjunctions, particles and other parts of speech.

2. Word Order In Japanese, predicates always come at the end of a sentence. Modifiers always appear in front of the word(s) modified.

3. Predicates Predicates are formed from verbs, adjectives, nouns and desu (da). They inflect according to, for example, whether they are (1) affirmative or negative, (2) past or non-past. They do not inflect for person, gender or number.

4. Particles Particles are used after a word or at the end of a sentence. They indicate relationships between words and add various meanings.

5. Omission Subjects and objects are often omitted if they can be understood from the context.

JAPANESE WRITING

There are three types of script in Japanese: hiragana, katakana, and kanji (Chinese characters).

Hiragana and katakana are phonetic symbols purely representing sounds, while kanji are ideographs, conveying meanings as well as sounds.

Japanese is usually written with a combination of hiragana, katakana, and kanji, with katakana used to write foreign names and loanwords and hiragana used to write particles and the grammatical endings of verbs and adjectives.

Romaji (the letters of the Roman alphabet) are also occasionally used to write Japanese (the names of train stations are one example) for the convenience of foreigners.

Here are examples of all four types of script:

田中 さん は ミラー さん と デパート へ 行 きます。
○　□　□　△　□　□　△　□　○　□

Mr. Tanaka is going to the department store with Mr. Miller.

大阪　Osaka
○　☆

(○－kanji　□－hiragana　△－katakana　☆－romaji)

INTRODUCTION

I. Japanese Pronunciation

1. Kana and Mora

Japanese can be written phonetically in kana as shown below.

A 'mora' is a unit of sound equivalent in length to one Japanese kana (or two of the contracted sounds called yo-on, which are written with small kana).

The Japanese language is based on five vowel sounds: a, i, u, e and o, which are used alone or attached to either a consonant (e.g. k + a = ka) or to a consonant plus the semi-vowel 'y' (e.g. k + y + a = kya) (the only exception being a special mora, n, which is not followed by a vowel). All of these sounds are or more or less equal in length when spoken.

e.g.,

```
          ┌── hiragana
  あ ア ───── katakana
  a  ───── romaji
```

	a-column	i-column	u-column	e-column	o-column
a-row a	あ ア a	い イ i	う ウ u	え エ e	お オ o
ka-row k	か カ ka	き キ ki	く ク ku	け ケ ke	こ コ ko
sa-row s	さ サ sa	し シ shi	す ス su	せ セ se	そ ソ so
ta-row t	た タ ta	ち チ chi	つ ツ tsu	て テ te	と ト to
na-row n	な ナ na	に ニ ni	ぬ ヌ nu	ね ネ ne	の ノ no
ha-row h	は ハ ha	ひ ヒ hi	ふ フ fu	へ ヘ he	ほ ホ ho
ma-row m	ま マ ma	み ミ mi	む ム mu	め メ me	も モ mo
ya-row y	や ヤ ya	(い イ) (i)	ゆ ユ yu	(え エ) (e)	よ ヨ yo
ra-row r	ら ラ ra	り リ ri	る ル ru	れ レ re	ろ ロ ro
wa-row w	わ ワ wa	(い イ) (i)	(う ウ) (u)	(え エ) (e)	を ヲ o
	ん ン n				

きゃ キャ kya	きゅ キュ kyu	きょ キョ kyo
しゃ シャ sha	しゅ シュ shu	しょ ショ sho
ちゃ チャ cha	ちゅ チュ chu	ちょ チョ cho
にゃ ニャ nya	にゅ ニュ nyu	にょ ニョ nyo
ひゃ ヒャ hya	ひゅ ヒュ hyu	ひょ ヒョ hyo
みゃ ミャ mya	みゅ ミュ myu	みょ ミョ myo

りゃ リャ rya	りゅ リュ ryu	りょ リョ ryo

	a-column	i-column	u-column	e-column	o-column
ga-row g	が ガ ga	ぎ ギ gi	ぐ グ gu	げ ゲ ge	ご ゴ go
za-row z	ざ ザ za	じ ジ ji	ず ズ zu	ぜ ゼ ze	ぞ ゾ zo
da-row d	だ ダ da	ぢ ヂ ji	づ ヅ zu	で デ de	ど ド do
ba-row b	ば バ ba	び ビ bi	ぶ ブ bu	べ ベ be	ぼ ボ bo
pa-row p	ぱ パ pa	ぴ ピ pi	ぷ プ pu	ぺ ペ pe	ぽ ポ po

ぎゃ ギャ gya	ぎゅ ギュ gyu	ぎょ ギョ gyo
じゃ ジャ ja	じゅ ジュ ju	じょ ジョ jo
びゃ ビャ bya	びゅ ビュ byu	びょ ビョ byo
ぴゃ ピャ pya	ぴゅ ピュ pyu	ぴょ ピョ pyo

The katakana letters in the square on the right are not in the above table. They are used to write sounds which are not original Japanese sounds but are needed for use in loanwords.

	ウィ wi		ウェ we	ウォ wo
			シェ she	
			チェ che	
ツァ tsa			ツェ tse	ツォ tso
	ティ ti	トゥ tu		
ファ fa	フィ fi		フェ fe	フォ fo
			ジェ je	
	ディ di	ドゥ du		
		デュ dyu		

2. Long vowels

The five vowel sounds mentioned earlier (a, i, u, e and o) constitute short vowels in Japanese, but they can be doubled in length (to two moras) to form long vowels. The meaning of a word changes according to the length of its vowel(s).

    e.g. obasan (aunt)：obāsan (grandmother)

          ojisan (uncle)：ojiisan (grandfather)

          yuki (snow)：yūki (courage)

          e (picture)：ē (yes)

          toru (take)：tōru (pass)

          koko (here)：kōkō (high school)

          heya (room)：heiya (plain)

          kādo (card) takushii (taxi) sūpā (supermarket)

          esukarētā (escalator) nōto (notebook)

[Note]

How to write long vowels in rōmaji:

In romanized transcription (rōmaji), a long vowel is marked by a bar above the letter as shown below, except for the long vowels of i and e which are written as ii and ei.

    Short vowel: a i u e o

    Long vowel: ā ii ū ei ō

*ē is used in some words such as:

  ē (yes) nē (I say) onēsan (elder sister)

*ē is also used to write loan words:

  kēki (cake)

3. Pronunciation of n

'n' is one mora long and never appears at the beginning of a word. To make it easier to say, it is pronounced /n/, /m/ or /ŋ/ according to the sound that comes after it.

① Before sounds from the 'ta-row', 'da-row', 'ra-row' and 'na-row',

  it is pronounced /n/,

    e.g. hantai (opposite) undō (sport) senro (track) minna (everyone).

② Before sounds from the 'ba-row', 'pa-row' and 'ma-row', it is pronounced /m/,

    e.g. shinbun (newspaper) enpitsu (pencil) unmei (destiny).

③ Before sounds from the 'ka-row' and 'ga-row', it is pronounced /ŋ/,

    e.g. tenki (weather) kengaku (study visit).

4. Double Consonants

Some consonants such as 'k', 's', 't' and 'p' occur as double consonants. In writing loan words, 'z' and 'd' also occur as double consonants.

    e.g. buka (subordinate) : bukka (commodity price)

          kasai (fire) : kassai (applause)

          oto (sound) : otto (husband)

          nikki (diary) zasshi (magazine) kitte (stamp)

          ippai (full) koppu (glass) beddo (bed)

5. Contracted Sound

The sound represented by using one of the small kana letters 'ゃ/ya', 'ゅ/yu' or 'ょ/yo' in combination with a full-sized kana letter is called a yo-on (contracted sound). Although written with two kana letters, these sounds are only one mora long.

    e.g. ひゃく hyaku (hundred) シャツ shatsu (shirt) おちゃ ocha (tea)

          しゅみ shumi (hobby) うんてんしゅ untenshu (driver)

          りょこう ryokō (travel) しやくしょ shiyakusho (city hall)

For Romanized transcription, see the table on the right on page3.

6. Pronunciation of ga-row

The consonants of the ga-row pronounced [g] when they fall at the beginning of a word, and [ŋ] when they fall elsewhere. However, some people these days make no distinction between these two sounds and pronounce them [g] wherever they fall.

7. Devoicing of vowels

The vowels [i] and [u] tend to be devoiced and become silent when they fall between voiceless consonants (e.g. suki like). The final vowel [u] of '∼ desu' and '-masu' also tends to be silent (e.g. shitai desu want to do, kikimasu listen).

8. Accent

The Japanese language has pitch accent; that is, some moras in a word are pronounced high and others low. There are four types of accent, and the meaning of a word changes according to how it is accented.

The standard Japanese accent is characterised by the fact that the first and second moras have different pitches, and that the pitch never rises again once it has fallen.

Types of accent

① Flat (the pitch does not drop)

    e.g. ni‾wa (garden) ha‾na (nose) na‾mae (name)

    Ni‾hon-go (Japanese language)

② Beginning high (the pitch drops after the first mora)

    e.g. ho‾|n (book) te‾|nki (weather) ra‾|igetsu (next month)

③ Middle high (the pitch drops after the second mora)

    e.g. ta‾ma|go (egg) hikōki [hi‾ko|oki] (aeroplane) se‾nse|i (teacher)

④ Ending high (the pitch drops after the last mora)

    e.g. ku‾tsu| (shoes) ha‾na| (flower) ya‾sumi| (holiday)

    o‾tōto| (younger brother)

ha‾na (nose) in ① and ha‾na| (flower) in ④ sound similar, but if the particle ga is added after these they are accented differently, and ① is pronounced ha‾na ga while ④ is pronounced ha‾na|ga. Here are some other examples of words whose meaning differs according to the type of accent:

    ha‾shi| (bridge) : ha‾shi (chopsticks)   i‾|chi (one) : i‾chi (position)

There are also local differences in accent. For example, the accent in the Osaka area is quite different from the standard accent. Here are some examples:

    e.g. Tokyo accent   :   Osaka accent

(standard Japanese accent)

          ha‾na| : ha‾na   (flower)

          ri‾|ngo : ri‾ngo   (apple)

          o‾|ngaku : o‾n|gaku (music)

9. Intonation

There are three patterns of intonation in Japanese: ① flat ② rising, and ③ falling. Questions are pronounced with a rising intonation. Other sentences are usually pronounced flat, but sometimes with a falling intonation. A falling intonation can express feelings such as agreement, disappointment, etc.

    e.g. Satō：   Ashita tomodachi to o-hanami o shimasu. 【→ flat】

                    Mirā-san mo issho ni ikimasen ka. 【↗ rising】

        Mirā：   Ii desu ne. 【↘ falling】

        Sato：   I'm going to see the cherry blossoms tomorrow with some friends.

                  Would you like to come with us, Mr. Miller?

        Miller：   That sounds good.

II. Classroom Language

1. Hajimemashō.　　　　　　　Let's begin.

2. Owarimashō.　　　　　　　Let's finish.

3. Yasumimashō.　　　　　　　Let's take a break.

4. Wakarimasu ka.　　　　　　Do you understand?

　　·····Hai, wakarimasu.　　　·····Yes, I do./

　　　　Iie, wakarimasen.　　　　　No, I don't.

5. Mō ichido [onegai-shimasu].　Once more [please].

6. Ii desu.　　　　　　　　　That's fine.

7. Chigaimasu.　　　　　　　No, that's wrong.

8. namae　　　　　　　　　name

9. shiken, shukudai　　　　　test, homework

10. shitsumon, kotae, rei　　　question, answer, example

III. Everyday Greetings and Expressions

1. Ohayō gozaimasu.　　　　Good morning.

2. Konnichiwa.　　　　　　　Hello.

3. Konbanwa.　　　　　　　Good evening.

4. Oyasuminasai.　　　　　　Good night.

5. Sayōnara.　　　　　　　　Goodbye.

6. Arigatō gozaimasu.　　　　Thank you.

7. Sumimasen.　　　　　　　Excuse me./Sorry.

8. Onegai-shimasu.　　　　　Please.

TERMS USED FOR INSTRUCTION

dai — ka	Lesson —	fōmu	form
bunkei	Sentence Pattern	-kei	~ form
reibun	Example Sentence	shūshoku	modification
kaiwa	Conversation	reigai	exception
renshū	Exercise		
mondai	Practice Question	meishi	noun
kotae	Answer	dōshi	verb
yomimono	Text	keiyōshi	adjective
fukushū	Review	i-keiyōshi	i-adjective
		na-keiyōshi	na-adjective
mokuji	Contents	joshi	particle
		fukushi	adverb
sakuin	Index	setsuzokushi	conjunction
		sūshi	numeral
bunpō	grammar	josūshi	counter suffix
bun	sentence	gimonshi	interrogative
tango (go)	word	meishi-bun	noun (predicate) sentence
ku	phrase		
setsu	clause	dōshi-bun	verb (predicate) sentence
hatsuon	pronunciation	keiyōshi-bun	adjective (predicate) sentence
boin	vowel		
shiin	consonant		
haku	mora	shugo	subject
akusento	accent	jutsugo	predicate
intonēshon	intonation	mokutekigo	object
		shudai	topic
[ka-]gyō	[ka-]row		
[i-]retsu	[i-]column	kōtei	affirmative
		hitei	negative
teinei-tai	polite style of speech	kanryō	perfective
futsū-tai	plain style of speech	mi-kanryō	imperfective
katsuyō	inflection, conjugation	kako	past
		hi-kako	non-past

KEY TO SYMBOLS AND ABBREVIATIONS

1. Symbols Used in I. Vocabulary

① ~ indicates a missing word or phrase

  e.g. ~ kara kimashita. came from ~

② Words and phrases that can be omitted are enclosed in square brackets:

  e.g. Dōzo yoroshiku [onegai-shimasu]. Pleased to meet you.

③ Synonymous words and phrases are enclosed in round brackets:

  e.g. dare (donata) who

④ Words marked with a star (✱) are not used in that lesson but are presented as being relevant.

⑤ The Exercise C section (**《Renshū C》**) presents expressions used in the lesson's Exercise C.

⑥ The Conversation section (**《Kaiwa》**) presents words and expressions used in the lesson's Conversation.

2. Abbreviations Used in IV. Grammar Notes

N	noun (meishi)	e.g. gakusei (student) tsukue (desk)
i-adj	i-adjective (i-keiyōshi)	e.g. oishii (delicious) takai (high, expensive)
na-adj	na-adjective (na-keiyōshi)	e.g. kirei[na] (beautiful) shizuka[na] (quiet)
V	verb (dōshi)	e.g. kakimasu (write) tabemasu (eat)
S	sentence (bun)	e.g. Kore wa hon desu. This is a book. Watashi wa ashita Tōkyō e ikimasu. I'm going to Tokyo tomorrow.

Lesson 1

1

I. Vocabulary

watashi	わたし	I
anata	あなた	you
ano hito (ano kata)	あの ひと（あの かた）	that person, he, she (ano kata is the polite equivalent of ano hito)
-san	〜さん	Mr., Ms. (suffix added to a name for expressing politeness)
-chan	〜ちゃん	(suffix often added to a child's name instead of -san)
-jin	〜じん	(suffix meaning 'a national of'; e.g. Amerika-jin, an American)
sensei	せんせい	teacher, instructor (not used when referring to one's own job)
kyōshi	きょうし	teacher, instructor
gakusei	がくせい	student
kaishain	かいしゃいん	company employee
shain	しゃいん	employee of 〜 company (used with a company's name, e.g. IMC no shain)
ginkōin	ぎんこういん	bank employee
isha	いしゃ	[medical] doctor
kenkyūsha	けんきゅうしゃ	researcher, scholar
daigaku	だいがく	university
byōin	びょういん	hospital
dare (donata)	だれ（どなた）	who (donata is the polite equivalent of dare)
-sai	ーさい	ー years old
nan-sai (o-ikutsu)	なんさい（おいくつ）	how old (o-ikutsu is the polite equivalent of nan-sai)
hai	はい	yes
iie	いいえ	no

10

⟨Renshū C⟩

Hajimemashite.	はじめまして。	How do you do? (lit. I am meeting you for the first time. Usually used as the first phrase when introducing oneself.)
～ kara kimashita.	～から きました。	I'm from ～ (country).
[Dōzo] yoroshiku [onegai-shimasu].	[どうぞ] よろしく [おねがいします]。	Pleased to meet you. (lit. Please be nice to me. Usually used at the end of a self-introduction.)
shitsurei desu ga	しつれいですが	Excuse me, but (used when asking someone for personal information such as their name or address)
O-namae wa?	おなまえは?	May I have your name?
Kochira wa -san desu.	こちらは ～さんです。	This is Mr./Ms. ～.

....

Amerika	アメリカ	U.S.A.
Igirisu	イギリス	U.K.
Indo	インド	India
Indoneshia	インドネシア	Indonesia
Kankoku	かんこく	South Korea
Tai	タイ	Thailand
Chūgoku	ちゅうごく	China
Doitsu	ドイツ	Germany
Nihon	にほん	Japan
Burajiru	ブラジル	Brazil

IMC/Pawā-denki/ Burajiru-eā	IMC／パワーでんき／ ブラジルエアー	fictitious companies
AKC	AKC	a fictitious institute
Kōbe-byōin	こうべびょういん	a fictitious hospital
Sakura-daigaku/ Fuji-daigaku	さくらだいがく／ ふじだいがく	fictitious universities

II. Translation

Sentence Patterns

1. I'm Mike Miller.
2. Mr. Santos isn't a student.
3. Is Mr. Miller a company employee?
4. Mr. Santos is also a company employee.

Example Sentences

1. Are you [Mr.] Mike Miller?
   ······Yes, I am [Mike Miller].

2. Are you a student, Mr. Miller?
   ······No, I'm not [a student].

3. Is Mr. Wang a bank employee?
   ······No, he isn't [a bank employee]. He's a doctor.

4. Who's that [person]?
   ······That's Professor Watt. He's at Sakura University.

5. Is Mr. Gupta a company employee?
   ······Yes, he is [a company employee].
   Is Karina a company employee, too?
   ······No, she's a student.

6. How old is Teresa?
   ······She's nine [years old].

Conversation

How do you do?

Sato: Good morning.

Yamada: Good morning.
           Ms. Sato, this is Mike Miller.

Miller: How do you do?
           I'm Mike Miller.
           I'm from America.
           Pleased to meet you.

Sato: I'm Keiko Sato.
           Nice to meet you.

III. Useful Words and Information

KUNI・HITO・KOTOBA　Countries, People and Languages

Kuni　Country	Hito　People	Kotoba　Language
Amerika (U.S.A.)	Amerika-jin	Eigo (English)
Igirisu (U.K.)	Igirisu-jin	Eigo (English)
Itaria (Italy)	Itaria-jin	Itaria-go (Italian)
Iran (Iran)	Iran-jin	Perushia-go (Persian)
Indo (India)	Indo-jin	Hindii-go (Hindi)
Indoneshia (Indonesia)	Indoneshia-jin	Indoneshia-go (Indonesian)
Ejiputo (Egypt)	Ejiputo-jin	Arabia-go (Arabic)
Ōsutoraria (Australia)	Ōsutoraria-jin	Eigo (English)
Kanada (Canada)	Kanada-jin	Eigo (English) Furansu-go (French)
Kankoku (South Korea)	Kankoku-jin	Kankoku-go (Korean)
Saujiarabia (Saudi Arabia)	Saujiarabia-jin	Arabia-go (Arabic)
Shingapōru (Singapore)	Shingapōru-jin	Eigo (English)
Supein (Spain)	Supein-jin	Supein-go (Spanish)
Tai (Thailand)	Tai-jin	Tai-go (Thai)
Chūgoku (China)	Chūgoku-jin	Chūgoku-go (Chinese)
Doitsu (Germany)	Doitsu-jin	Doitsu-go (German)
Nihon (Japan)	Nihon-jin	Nihon-go (Japanese)
Furansu (France)	Furansu-jin	Furansu-go (French)
Firipin (Philippines)	Firipin-jin	Firipino-go (Filipino)
Burajiru (Brazil)	Burajiru-jin	Porutogaru-go (Portuguese)
Betonamu (Vietnam)	Betonamu-jin	Betonamu-go (Vietnamese)
Marēshia (Malaysia)	Marēshia-jin	Marēshia-go (Malaysian)
Mekishiko (Mexico)	Mekishiko-jin	Supein-go (Spanish)
Roshia (Russia)	Roshia-jin	Roshia-go (Russian)

IV. Grammar Notes

1. | N₁ wa N₂ desu |

1) Particle wa

The particle wa indicates that the noun before it (N₁) is the topic of the sentence (see Topic and Subject article). The speaker forms a sentence by adding wa to what he or she wants to talk about, and then makes statements about it.

① Watashi wa Maiku Mirā desu.　　　　I'm Mike Miller.

2) Desu

Nouns used with desu work as predicates. Besides indicating judgment or assertion, desu also shows politeness towards the listener. Desu inflects when the sentence is negative (see 2. below) or in the past tense (see Lesson 12).

② Watashi wa kaishain desu.　　　　I'm a company employee.

2. | N₁ wa N₂ ja (dewa) arimasen |

Ja (dewa) arimasen is the negative form of desu. Ja arimasen is often used in everyday conversation, while dewa arimasen is used in formal speech and writing.

③ Santosu-san wa gakusei　ja　arimasen.　　Mr. Santos isn't a student.
　　　　　　　　　　(dewa)

3. | N₁ wa N₂ desu ka |　(question)

1) Particle ka

The particle ka is used to express uncertainty, doubt, etc. on the part of the speaker. A question can be formed simply by adding ka to the end of a sentence. A question usually ends with a rising intonation.

2) Questions asking whether a statement is correct or not

This type of question is formed simply by adding ka to the end of the statement, leaving the word order the same. The reply begins with hai if the statement is agreed with, and iie if it is disagreed with.

④ Mirā-san wa Amerika-jin desu ka.　　Is Mr. Miller an American?
　　·····Hai, Amerika-jin desu.　　　　·····Yes, he is [an American].

⑤ Mirā-san wa sensei desu ka.　　Is Mr. Miller a teacher?
　　·····Iie, sensei ja arimasen.　　　　·····No, he isn't [a teacher].

3) Questions with interrogatives

An interrogative replaces the part of the sentence that states what the speaker wants to ask about. The word order does not change, and ka is added at the end.

⑥ Ano kata wa donata desu ka.　　Who's that [person]?
　　·····[Ano kata wa] Mirā-san desu.　　·····That's Mr. Miller.

4. N mo

Mo is used when the same thing applies as was stated previously.

⑦   Mirā-san wa kaishain desu. Guputa-san mo kaishain desu.
   Mr. Miller is a company employee. Mr Gupta is also a company employee.

5. N₁ no N₂

When a noun N_1 modifies a following noun N_2, no is used to connect the two nouns.
In Lesson 1, N_1 represents an organisation or some kind of group to which N_2 belongs.

⑧   Mirā-san wa IMC no shain desu.   Mr. Miller is an IMC employee.

6. -san

-san is added to the given name or family name of the listener or a third person to
show the speaker's respect to that person. It should never be used with the speaker's
own name. -chan is added to small children's names instead of -san to indicate
familiarity.

⑨   Ano kata wa Mirā-san desu.   That's Mr. Miller.

When referring directly to the listener, the word anata (you) is not generally used if
the speaker knows the listener's name. The listener's given name or family name
followed by -san is usually used.

⑩   Suzuki: Mirā-san wa gakusei desu ka. Suzuki: Are you a student, Mr. Miller?
   Mirā: Iie, kaishain desu.   Miller: No, I work for a company.

[Note] Anata is used to address someone with whom one is very familiar, such as
one's husband, wife, romantic partner, etc. Be careful about using it in other situations,
as it can sound impolite.

Lesson 2

I. Vocabulary

kore	これ	this (thing here)
sore	それ	that (thing near the listener)
are	あれ	that (thing over there)
kono ~	この ~	this ~, this ~ here
sono ~*	その ~	that ~, that ~ near the listener
ano ~*	あの ~	that ~, that ~ over there
hon	ほん	book
jisho	じしょ	dictionary
zasshi	ざっし	magazine
shinbun	しんぶん	newspaper
nōto	ノート	notebook
techō	てちょう	personal organiser
meishi	めいし	business card
kādo	カード	(credit) card
enpitsu	えんぴつ	pencil
bōrupen	ボールペン	ballpoint pen
shāpu-penshiru	シャープペンシル	mechanical pencil, propelling pencil
kagi	かぎ	key
tokei	とけい	watch, clock
kasa	かさ	umbrella
kaban	かばん	bag, briefcase
CD	CD	CD, compact disc
terebi	テレビ	television
rajio	ラジオ	radio
kamera	カメラ	camera
konpyūtā	コンピューター	computer
kuruma	くるま	car, vehicle
tsukue	つくえ	desk
isu	いす	chair
chokorēto	チョコレート	chocolate
kōhii	コーヒー	coffee

[o-]miyage	[お]みやげ	souvenir, present
Eigo	えいご	the English language
Nihon-go	にほんご	the Japanese language
-go	～ご	～ language
nan	なん	what
sō	そう	so

〈Renshū C〉

anō	あのう	Er... (used to show hesitation)
e	えっ	Oh? What! (used when hearing something unexpected)
Dōzo.	どうぞ。	Here you are. (used when offering someone something)
[Dōmo] arigatō [gozaimasu].	[どうも] ありがとう [ございます]。	Thank you [very much].
Sō desu ka.	そうですか。	I see.
Chigaimasu.	ちがいます。	No, it isn't./You are wrong.
a	あ	Oh! (used when becoming aware of something)

〈Kaiwa〉

Korekara osewa ni narimasu.	これから おせわに なります。	Thank you in advance for your kindness.
Kochira koso [dōzo] yoroshiku [onegai-shimasu].	こちらこそ [どうぞ] よろしく [おねがい します]。	Pleased to meet you, too. (response to [Dōzo] yoroshiku [onegai-shimasu].)

2

17

II. Translation

Sentence Patterns
1. This is a dictionary.
2. That's my umbrella.
3. This book is mine.

Example Sentences

1. Is this a ballpoint pen?
   ⋯⋯Yes, it is.

2. Is that a notebook?
   ⋯⋯No, it's a personal organiser.

3. What's that?
   ⋯⋯It's a business card.

4. Is this a 9, or a 7?
   ⋯⋯It's a 9.

5. What kind of magazine is that?
   ⋯⋯It's a computer magazine.

6. Whose bag is that?
   ⋯⋯It's Ms. Sato's [bag].

7. Is this yours, Mr. Miller?
   ⋯⋯No, it's not [mine].

8. Whose is this key?
   ⋯⋯It's mine.

Conversation

Thank you in advance for your kindness

Ichiro Yamada:	Yes, who is it?
Santos:	It's Jose Santos, from 408.

⋯⋯⋯⋯⋯⋯⋯⋯⋯⋯⋯⋯⋯⋯⋯⋯⋯⋯⋯⋯⋯⋯⋯⋯⋯⋯⋯

Santos:	Hello, I'm Jose Santos.
	I've just moved in here. (lit: Thank you in advance for your kindness.)
	Nice to meet you.
Ichiro Yamada:	Pleased to meet you, too.
Santos:	Here's some coffee for you. (lit: Umm...... this is coffee. Please take it.)
Ichiro Yamada:	Thank you very much.

III. Useful Words and Information

NAMAE   Family Names

Common Family Names in Japanese

1	Satō	2	Suzuki	3	Takahashi	4	Tanaka
5	Watanabe	6	Itō	7	Yamamoto	8	Nakamura
9	Kobayashi	10	Katō	11	Yoshida	12	Yamada
13	Sasaki	14	Saitō	15	Yamaguchi	16	Matsumoto
17	Inoue	18	Kimura	19	Hayashi	20	Shimizu

城岡啓二、村山忠重「日本の姓の全国順位データベース」より。2011 年 8 月公開
Taken from 'A Database of the Nationwide Order of Prevalence of Japanese Family Names',
by Keiji Shirooka and Tadashige Murayama August 2011

Greetings

Hajimemashite.

⇦ When people meet for the first time on business, business cards are exchanged.

Dōzo yoroshiku onegai-shimasu.

When you move house, it is polite to introduce yourself to your new neighbours and give them a ⇨ small gift, such as a towel, soap or sweets.

IV. Grammar Notes

1. kore/sore/are

Kore, sore and are are demonstratives and work as nouns.

Kore refers to something near the speaker.

Sore refers to something near the listener.

Are refers to something distant from both the speaker and the listener.

① Sore wa jisho desu ka.   Is that a dictionary?

② Kore wa dare no kasa desu ka.   Whose umbrella is this?

2. kono N/sono N/ano N

Kono, sono and ano modify nouns.

③ Kono hon wa watashi no desu.   This book is mine.

④ Ano kata wa donata desu ka.   Who is that [person]?

kore
kono kaban

sore
sono kaban

are
ano kaban

3. sō desu

In a noun sentence, the word sō is often used to answer (in the affirmative) a question requiring an affirmative or negative answer. The expression hai, sō desu. can be used.

⑤ Sore wa jisho desu ka.   Is that a dictionary?

    ······Hai, sō desu.   ······Yes, it is.

Sō is not usually used when answering a question in the negative; it is more common to say chigaimasu (No, it isn't), followed by the correct answer.

⑥ Sore wa Mirā-san no desu ka.   Is that Mr. Miller's?

    ······Iie, chigaimasu.   ······No, it isn't.

⑦ Sore wa shāpu-penshiru desu ka.   Is that a mechanical pencil?

    ······Iie, bōrupen desu.   ······No, it's a ballpoint pen.

4. ~ ka, ~ ka

This is a question asking the listener to choose between two or more alternatives for the answer. In answering this type of question, it is usual to state the chosen alternative, without saying either hai or iie.

⑧   Kore wa "9" desu ka, "7" desu ka.   Is this a 9 or a 7?

      ······ "9" desu.   ······It's a 9.

5. N₁ no N₂

It was explained in Lesson 1 that no is used to connect two nouns N₁ and N₂ when N₁ modifies N₂. The present lesson explains some other uses of no.

1) N₁ explains what N₂ is about.

   ⑨   Kore wa konpyūtā no hon desu.   This is a book on computers.

2) N₁ indicates who owns N₂.

   ⑩   Kore wa watashi no hon desu.   This is my book.

6. no substituting for a noun

No can be used instead of a noun that has already been mentioned (e.g. instead of kaban in example ⑪). If placed after the noun (as in example ⑪, where it comes after the noun Satō-san), it enables N₂ (kaban) in N₁ no N₂ (Satō-san no kaban) to be omitted. No is used as a replacement for things but not for people.

⑪   Are wa dare no kaban desu ka.   Whose bag is that?

     ······Satō-san no desu.   ······It's Ms. Sato's.

⑫   Kono kaban wa anata no desu ka.   Is this bag yours?

     ······Iie, watashi no ja arimasen.   ······No, it isn't [mine].

⑬   Mirā-san wa IMC no shain desu ka.   Does Mr. Miller work at IMC?

     ······Hai, IMC no shain desu.   ······Yes, he does.

    ×   Hai, IMC no desu.

7. o-

The prefix o- is attached to words when the speaker is speaking politely (e.g. [o-]miyage, [o-]sake).

8. sō desu ka

This expression is used by the speaker to acknowledge some new information he or she has just been given. It is pronounced with a falling intonation.

⑭   Kono kasa wa anata no desu ka.   Is this umbrella yours?

     ······Iie, chigaimasu. Shumitto-san no desu.   ······No, it isn't. It's Mr Schmidt's.

     Sō desu ka.   Oh, I see.

Lesson 3

I. Vocabulary

koko	ここ	here, this place
soko	そこ	there, that place near the listener
asoko	あそこ	that place over there
doko	どこ	where, what place
kochira	こちら	this way, this place (polite equivalent of koko)
sochira	そちら	that way, that place near the listener (polite equivalent of soko)
achira	あちら	that way, that place over there (polite equivalent of asoko)
dochira	どちら	which way, where (polite equivalent of doko)
kyōshitsu	きょうしつ	classroom
shokudō	しょくどう	dining hall, canteen
jimusho	じむしょ	office
kaigishitsu	かいぎしつ	conference room, meeting room
uketsuke	うけつけ	reception desk
robii	ロビー	lobby
heya	へや	room
toire (otearai)	トイレ（おてあらい）	toilet, rest room
kaidan	かいだん	staircase
erebētā	エレベーター	lift, elevator
esukarētā	エスカレーター	escalator
jidō-hanbaiki	じどうはんばいき	vending machine
denwa	でんわ	telephone handset, telephone call
[o-]kuni	［お］くに	country
kaisha	かいしゃ	company
uchi	うち	house, home

kutsu	くつ	shoes
nekutai	ネクタイ	tie, necktie
wain	ワイン	wine
uriba	うりば	department, counter (in a department store, etc.)
chika	ちか	basement
-kai (-gai)	一かい（一がい）	-th floor
nan-gai*	なんがい	what floor
-en	一えん	一 yen
ikura	いくら	how much
hyaku	ひゃく	hundred
sen	せん	thousand
man	まん	ten thousand

〈Renshū C〉

Sumimasen.	すみません。	Excuse me.
Dōmo.	どうも。	Thanks.

〈Kaiwa〉

Irasshaimase.	いらっしゃいませ。	Welcome./May I help you? (a greeting to a customer or a guest entering a shop, etc.)
[〜 o] misete kudasai.	［〜を］みせて ください。	Please show me [〜].
ja	じゃ	well, then, in that case
[〜 o] kudasai.	［〜を］ください。	Give me [〜], please.

....

Itaria	イタリア	Italy
Suisu	スイス	Switzerland
Furansu	フランス	France
Jakaruta	ジャカルタ	Jakarta
Bankoku	バンコク	Bangkok
Berurin	ベルリン	Berlin
Shin-Ōsaka	しんおおさか	name of a station in Osaka

II. Translation

Sentence Patterns

1. This is the cafeteria.
2. The elevator's over there.

Example Sentences

1. Is this Shin-Osaka?

   ······Yes, it is.

2. Where's the toilet?

   ······It's over there.

3. Where's Mr. Yamada?

   ······He's in the meeting room.

4. Where's the office?

   ······It's over there.

5. Which country are you from?

   ······America.

6. Where are those shoes from?

   ······They're Italian [shoes].

7. How much is this watch?

   ······It's 18,600 yen.

Conversation

I'll take it, please

Shop Assistant A:	Good afternoon. (lit: Welcome.)
Maria:	[Excuse me.] Where's the wine department?
Shop Assistant A:	It's on Basement Level 1.
Maria:	Thanks.

···

Maria:	Excuse me. Could you show me that bottle of wine, please?
Shop Assistant B:	Yes, here you are.
Maria:	Where's this wine from?
Shop Assistant B:	It's from Japan.
Maria:	How much is it?
Shop Assistant B:	It's 2,500 yen.
Maria:	OK, I'll take it, please.

3

III. Useful Words and Information

DEPĀTO   Department Store

3

okujō	yūenchi amusement area
8-kai	resutoran・moyōshimono-kaijō restaurants, event hall
7-kai	tokei・megane watches, spectacles
6-kai	supōtsu-yōhin・ryokō-yōhin sporting goods, leisure goods
5-kai	kodomo-fuku・omocha・hon・bunbōgu children's clothes, toys, books, stationery
4-kai	kagu・shokki・denka-seihin furniture, kitchenware, electrical appliances
3-gai	shinshi-fuku men's wear
2-kai	fujin-fuku ladies' wear
1-kai	kutsu・kaban・akusesarii・keshōhin shoes, bags, accessories, cosmetics
Chika 1-kai	shokuhin food
Chika 2-kai	chūshajō car park, parking lot

25

IV. Grammar Notes

1. koko/soko/asoko/kochira/sochira/achira

The demonstratives koko, soko and asoko refer to places. Koko indicates the place where the speaker is, soko the place where the listener is, and asoko a place distant from both the speaker and the listener. Kochira, sochira and achira refer to direction and can also be used as politer-sounding alternatives for koko, soko and asoko.

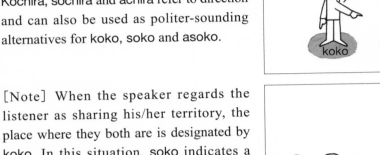

[Note] When the speaker regards the listener as sharing his/her territory, the place where they both are is designated by koko. In this situation, soko indicates a place slightly distant from where they both are, and asoko somewhere even further away.

2. N wa place desu

Using this sentence pattern, you can state where a place, thing or person is.

① Otearai wa asoko desu.   The toilet is over there.

② Denwa wa 2-kai desu.   The telephone is on the second floor.

③ Yamada-san wa jimusho desu.   Mr. Yamada is in his office.

3. doko/dochira

Doko is used for asking "Where?" and dochira for "Which direction?" Dochira can also be used for asking "Where?", in which case it is politer than doko.

④ Otearai wa doko desu ka.   Where's the toilet?
    ······Asoko desu.   ······It's over there.

⑤ Erebēta wa dochira desu ka.   Where's the lift?
    ······Achira desu.   ······It's in that direction. (It's over there.)

Doko and dochira are also used for asking the name of the country, company, school or other place or organisation to which someone belongs. Nan cannot be used in this case. Dochira is politer than doko.

⑥ Gakkō wa doko desu ka.　　What school do you go to?

⑦ Kaisha wa dochira desu ka.　　What company do you work for?

4. N_1 no N_2

When N_1 is the name of a country and N_2 is the name of a product, it means that N_2 is made in that country. When N_1 is the name of a company and N_2 is the name of a product, it means that N_2 is made by that company. The interrogative doko is used when asking where or by what company something is made.

⑧ Kore wa doko no konpyūta desu ka.　　Where is this computer made? / What company is this computer made by?

‥‥‥Nihon no konpyūta desu.　　‥‥‥It's made in Japan.
‥‥‥Pawā-denki no konpyūta desu.
‥‥‥It's made by Power Electric Company.

5. The ko/so/a/do system of demonstratives

	ko series	so series	a series	do series
Thing	kore	sore	are	dore (L .16)
Thing/Person	kono N	sono N	ano N	dono N (L .16)
Place	koko	soko	asoko	doko
Direction/ Place (polite)	kochira	sochira	achira	dochira

6. o-

The prefix o- is added to things related to the listener or a third party in order to show the speaker's respect toward that person.

⑨ [O-]kuni wa dochira desu ka.　　What country are you from?

Lesson 4

I. Vocabulary

okimasu	おきます	get up, wake up
nemasu	ねます	sleep, go to bed
hatarakimasu	はたらきます	work
yasumimasu	やすみます	take a rest, take a holiday
benkyō-shimasu	べんきょうします	study
owarimasu	おわります	finish
depāto	デパート	department store
ginkō	ぎんこう	bank
yūbinkyoku	ゆうびんきょく	post office
toshokan	としょかん	library
bijutsukan	びじゅつかん	art museum, art gallery
ima	いま	now
-ji	ーじ	ー o'clock
-fun (-pun)	ーふん（ーぷん）	ー minute
han	はん	half
nan-ji	なんじ	what time
nan-pun*	なんぷん	what minute
gozen	ごぜん	a.m., morning
gogo	ごご	p.m., afternoon
asa	あさ	morning
hiru	ひる	daytime, noon
ban (yoru)	ばん（よる）	night, evening
ototoi	おととい	the day before yesterday
kinō	きのう	yesterday
kyō	きょう	today
ashita	あした	tomorrow
asatte	あさって	the day after tomorrow
kesa	けさ	this morning
konban	こんばん	this evening, tonight
yasumi	やすみ	rest, a holiday, a day off
hiruyasumi	ひるやすみ	lunchtime

shiken	しけん	examination, test
kaigi	かいぎ	meeting, conference （〜 o shimasu : hold a meeting）
eiga	えいが	film, movie
maiasa	まいあさ	every morning
maiban	まいばん	every night
mainichi	まいにち	every day
getsu-yōbi	げつようび	Monday
ka-yōbi	かようび	Tuesday
sui-yōbi	すいようび	Wednesday
moku-yōbi	もくようび	Thursday
kin-yōbi	きんようび	Friday
do-yōbi	どようび	Saturday
nichi-yōbi	にちようび	Sunday
nan-yōbi	なんようび	what day of the week
〜 kara	〜から	from 〜
〜 made	〜まで	up to 〜, until 〜
〜 to 〜	〜と 〜	and （used to connect nouns）

4

29

〈Renshū C〉

Taihen desu ne.	たいへんですね。	That's tough, isn't it? （used when expressing sympathy）

〈Kaiwa〉

bangō	ばんごう	number
nan-ban	なんばん	what number
sochira	そちら	your place

....

Nyūyōku	ニューヨーク	New York
Pekin	ペキン	Beijing （北京）
Rosanzerusu	ロサンゼルス	Los Angeles
Rondon	ロンドン	London
Asuka	あすか	a fictitious Japanese restaurant
Appuru-ginkō	アップルぎんこう	a fictitious bank
Midori-toshokan	みどりとしょかん	a fictitious library
Yamato-bijutsukan	やまとびじゅつかん	a fictitious art gallery

II. Translation

Sentence Patterns

1. It's five past four now.
2. I get up at six [o'clock] every morning.
3. I studied yesterday.

Example Sentences

1. What time is it now?
   ······It's ten past two.
   What's the time in New York now?
   ······It's ten past midnight.

2. What days are you off work?
   ······Saturdays and Sundays.

3. What are Apple Bank's opening hours?
   ······From nine till three.

4. What time do you usually go to bed?
   ······[I go to bed at] eleven o'clock.

5. When do you start and finish studying every day?
   ······I study from nine am until three pm.

6. Do you work on Saturdays?
   ······No, I don't.

7. Did you study yesterday?
   ······No, I didn't.

Conversation

What time are you open to?

Miller:	Excuse me, what is Asuka's phone number?
Sato:	Asuka? It's 5275-2725.
Miller:	Thank you very much.

···

'Asuka' staff member:	Hello, Asuka here.
Miller:	Excuse me. What time are you open to?
'Asuka' staff member:	Until ten.
Miller:	What days of the week are you closed?
'Asuka' staff member:	Sundays.
Miller:	I see. Thank you.

III. Useful Words and Information

DENWA · TEGAMI　Telephone and Letters

How to Use a Public Telephone

① Lift the receiver.　② Put coins or a card into the slot.　③ Press the numbers.*　④ Hang up the receiver.　⑤ Take card or change (if any).

Public telephones accept only ¥10 coins, ¥100 coins, and telephone cards.
If you put in a ¥100 coin, no change will be returned.
* If the machine has a start button, press it after ③ .

Emergency and Information Numbers

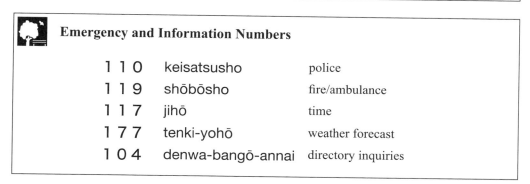

1 1 0	keisatsusho	police
1 1 9	shōbōsho	fire/ambulance
1 1 7	jihō	time
1 7 7	tenki-yohō	weather forecast
1 0 4	denwa-bangō-annai	directory inquiries

How to Write an Address

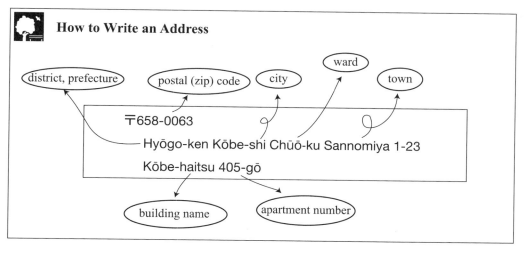

district, prefecture　postal (zip) code　city　ward　town

〒658-0063
Hyōgo-ken Kōbe-shi Chūō-ku Sannomiya 1-23
Kōbe-haitsu 405-gō

building name　apartment number

IV. Grammar Notes

1. Ima –ji –fun desu

To express time, the counter suffixes -ji (o'clock) and -fun(-pun) (minutes) are placed after the numbers. -fun is used after 2, 5, 7, or 9 and -pun after 1, 3, 4, 6, 8 and 10. 1, 6, 8 and 10 are read ip(-pun), rop(-pun), hap(-pun) and jup/jip(-pun) (see Appendix).
To ask the time, nan is placed in front of -ji or -pun.

①   Ima nan-ji desu ka.   What time is it now?
      ······7-ji 10-pun desu.   ······It's 7:10.

2. V-masu/V-masen/V-mashita/V-masendeshita

1) V-masu works as a predicate. Using masu shows politeness toward the listener.

②   Watashi wa mainichi benkyō-shimasu.   I study every day.

2) V-masu is used when a sentence expresses something habitual or a truth. It is also used when a sentence expresses a behavior or event that will occur in the future. The table below shows its negative and past-tense forms.

	Non-past (future/present)	Past
Affirmative	okimasu	okimashita
Negative	okimasen	okimasendeshita

③   Maiasa 6-ji ni okimasu.   I get up at six every morning.

④   Ashita 6-ji ni okimasu.   I'm going to get up at six tomorrow morning.

⑤   Kesa 6-ji ni okimashita.   I got up at six this morning.

3) Verb question sentences are formed by putting ka at the end of the sentence, without changing the word order. When using an interrogative, this is placed in the part of the sentence that the speaker wants to ask about. When answering such questions, the verb in the question is repeated. Sō desu and chigaimasu (see Lesson 2) cannot be used when replying to a verb sentence question.

⑥   Kinō benkyō-shimashita ka.   Did you study yesterday?
      ······Hai, benkyō-shimashita.   ······Yes, I did [study].
      ······Iie, benkyō-shimasendeshita. ······No, I didn't [study].

⑦   Maiasa nan-ji ni okimasu ka.   What time do you get up in the mornings?
      ······6-ji ni okimasu.   ······[I get up at] six o'clock.

3. N (time) ni V

The particle ni is appended to a noun indicating time to indicate the time of occurrence of an action.

⑧   6-ji han ni okimasu.   I get up at six-thirty.

⑨　7-gatsu futsuka ni Nihon e kimashita.

I came to Japan on the second of July. (See Lesson 5.)

[Note 1] Ni is not used with the following kinds of noun expressing time:

kyō, ashita, asatte, kinō, ototoi, kesa, konban, ima, maiasa, maiban, mainichi, senshū (L.5), konshū (L.5), raishū (L.5), itsu (L.5), sengetsu (L.5), kongetsu (L.5), raigetsu (L.5), kotoshi (L.5), rainen (L.5), kyonen (L.5), etc.

⑩　Kinō benkyō-shimashita.　　　　　　I studied yesterday.

[Note 2] With the following nouns, the use of ni is optional:

-yōbi, asa, hiru, ban, yoru

⑪　Nichi-yōbi [ni] Nara e ikimasu.

I'm going to Nara on Sunday. (See Lesson 5.)

4.　　N₁ kara　N₂ made

1)　Kara indicates a starting time or place, and made indicates a finishing time or place.

⑫　9-ji kara 5-ji made benkyō-shimasu.　　I study from 9 to 5.

⑬　Ōsaka kara Tōkyō made 3-jikan kakarimasu.

It takes three hours from Osaka to Tokyo. (See Lesson 11.)

2)　Kara and made are not always used together.

⑭　9-ji kara hatarakimasu.　　　　　I start work at nine.

3)　To indicate the starting or finishing time/date of a noun introduced as a topic, ～ kara, ～ made, or ～ kara ～ made can be used with 'desu' attached.

⑮　Ginkō wa 9-ji kara 3-ji made desu.　　The bank's open from 9 to 3.

⑯　Hiruyasumi wa 12-ji kara desu.　　The lunch break starts at 12.

5.　　N₁ to　N₂

The particle to connects two nouns in coordinate relation.

⑰　Ginkō no yasumi wa do-yōbi to nichi-yōbi desu.

The bank is closed on Saturdays and Sundays.

6.　　～ ne

The particle ne is attached to the end of a sentence and is used to elicit agreement from the listener, check that the listener has understood, or emphasize something to the listener.

⑱　Mainichi 10-ji made benkyō-shimasu.　I study till ten every day.
　　……Taihen desu ne.　　　　　　　……That's tough, isn't it?

⑲　Yamada-san no denwa-bangō wa 871 no 6813 desu.

Mr. Yamada's telephone number is 871-6813.

　　……871 no 6813 desu ne.　　　　……871-6813, right?

4

Lesson 5

I. Vocabulary

ikimasu	いきます	go
kimasu	きます	come
kaerimasu	かえります	go home, return
gakkō	がっこう	school
sūpā	スーパー	supermarket
eki	えき	station
hikōki	ひこうき	aeroplane, airplane
fune	ふね	ship
densha	でんしゃ	electric train
chikatetsu	ちかてつ	underground, subway
shinkansen	しんかんせん	the Shinkansen, the bullet train
basu	バス	bus
takushii	タクシー	taxi
jitensha	じてんしゃ	bicycle
aruite	あるいて	on foot
hito	ひと	person, people
tomodachi	ともだち	friend
kare*	かれ	he, boyfriend, lover
kanojo	かのじょ	she, girlfriend, lover
kazoku	かぞく	family
hitori de	ひとりで	alone, by oneself
senshū	せんしゅう	last week
konshū	こんしゅう	this week
raishū	らいしゅう	next week
sengetsu	せんげつ	last month
kongetsu*	こんげつ	this month
raigetsu	らいげつ	next month
kyonen	きょねん	last year
kotoshi*	ことし	this year
rainen	らいねん	next year
-nen*	ーねん	-th year
nan-nen*	なんねん	what year
-gatsu	ーがつ	-th month of the year
nan-gatsu*	なんがつ	what month

tsuitachi	ついたち	first day of the month	
futsuka*	ふつか	second, two days	
mikka	みっか	third, three days	
yokka*	よっか	fourth, four days	
itsuka*	いつか	fifth, five days	
muika	むいか	sixth, six days	
nanoka*	なのか	seventh, seven days	
yōka*	ようか	eighth, eight days	
kokonoka	ここのか	ninth, nine days	
tōka	とおか	tenth, ten days	
jū yokka	じゅうよっか	fourteenth, fourteen days	
hatsuka*	はつか	twentieth, twenty days	
ni-jū yokka*	にじゅうよっか	twenty-fourth, twenty-four days	
-nichi	ーにち	-th day of the month, ー day(s)	
nan-nichi*	なんにち	which day of the month, how many days	
itsu	いつ	when	
tanjōbi	たんじょうび	birthday	

〈Renshū C〉

Sō desu ne.	そうですね。	Yes, it is.

〈Kaiwa〉

[Dōmo] arigatō gozaimashita.	[どうも] ありがとう ございました。	Thank you very much.
Dō itashimashite.	どう いたしまして。	You're welcome./Don't mention it.
-bansen	ーばんせん	platform ー , -th platform
tsugi no	つぎの	next
futsū	ふつう	local (train)
kyūkō*	きゅうこう	rapid
tokkyū*	とっきゅう	express

··

Kōshien	こうしえん	name of a town near Osaka
Ōsakajō	おおさかじょう	Osaka Castle, a famous castle in Osaka

5

· 35

II. Translation

Sentence Patterns
1. I [am going to] go to Kyoto.
2. I [am going to] go home by taxi.
3. I came to Japan with my family.

Example Sentences
1. Where are you going tomorrow?
   ······[I'm going] to Nara.

2. Where did you go on Sunday?
   ······I didn't go anywhere.

3. How are you getting to Tokyo?
   ······[I'm going] on the bullet train.

4. Who are you going to Tokyo with?
   ······[I'm going with] Mr. Yamada.

5. When did you arrive in Japan?
   ······[I arrived] on the twenty-fifth of March.

6. When's your birthday?
   ······[It's on] the thirteenth of June.

Conversation
Does this train go to Koshien?

Santos:	Excuse me. How much is it to Koshien?
Woman:	It's 350 yen.
Santos:	350 yen? Thank you.
Woman:	You're welcome.

Santos:	Excuse me, which platform for Koshien, please?
Station attendant:	Number 5.
Santos:	Thanks.

Santos:	Excuse me, does this train go to Koshien?
Man:	No, the next local train does.
Santos:	Oh, I see. Thanks.

III. Useful Words and Information

SHUKUSAIJITSU   National Holidays

1-gatsu tsuitachi	Ganjitsu	New Year's Day
1-gatsu dai-2 getsu-yōbi**	Seijin no hi	Coming-of-Age Day
2-gatsu 11-nichi	Kenkoku kinen no hi	National Foundation Day
3-gatsu hatsuka*	Shunbun no hi	Vernal Equinox Day
4-gatsu 29-nichi	Shōwa no hi	Showa Day
5-gatsu mikka	Kenpō kinenbi	Constitution Memorial Day
5-gatsu yokka	Midori no hi	Greenery Day
5-gatsu itsuka	Kodomo no hi	Children's Day
7-gatsu dai-3 getsu-yōbi***	Umi no hi	Marine Day
8-gatsu 11-nichi	Yama no hi	Mountain Day
9-gatsu dai-3 getsu-yōbi***	Keirō no hi	Respect-for-the-Aged Day
9-gatsu 23-nichi*	Shūbun no hi	Autumnal Equinox Day
10-gatsu dai-2 getsu-yōbi**	Taiiku no hi	Health and Sports Day
11-gatsu mikka	Bunka no hi	Culture Day
11-gatsu 23-nichi	Kinrō-kansha no hi	Labour Thanksgiving Day
12-gatsu 23-nichi	Tennō-tanjōbi	The Emperor's Birthday

* Varies from year to year.

** The second Monday

*** The third Monday

 If a national holiday falls on a Sunday, the following Monday is taken off instead. The week from 29th April to 5th May, which contains a series of holidays, is called Gōruden-uiiku (Golden Week). Some companies make the whole of this week a holiday for their employees.

IV. Grammar Notes

1. N (place) e ikimasu/kimasu/kaerimasu

When a verb indicates movement to a certain place, the particle e is put after the place noun to show the direction of the move.

①	Kyōto e ikimasu.	I'm going to Kyoto.
②	Nihon e kimashita.	I came to Japan.
③	Uchi e kaerimasu.	I'm going home.

2. Doko [e] mo ikimasen/ikimasendeshita

When you want to deny everything covered by an interrogative, you attach the particle mo to the interrogative and put the verb in its negative form.

④	Doko [e] mo ikimasen.	I'm not going anywhere.
⑤	Nani mo tabemasen.	I'm not going to eat anything. (See Lesson 6.)
⑥	Dare mo kimasendeshita.	Nobody came.

3. N (vehicle) de ikimasu/kimasu/kaerimasu

The particle de indicates a means or method. The speaker attaches it after a noun representing a vehicle and uses it together with a movement verb to indicate his or her means of transport.

⑦	Densha de ikimasu.	I'm going by train.
⑧	Takushii de kimashita.	I came by taxi.

When talking about walking somewhere, the speaker uses the expression aruite. In this case, the particle de is not used.

⑨	Eki kara aruite kaerimashita.	I walked home from the station.

4. N (person/animal) to V

When talking about doing something with a person or an animal, the person or animal is marked with the particle to.

⑩	Kazoku to Nihon e kimashita.	I came to Japan with my family.

If doing something by oneself, the expression hitori de is used. In this case, the particle to is not used.

⑪	Hitori de Tōkyō e ikimasu.	I'm going to Tokyo on my own.

5. itsu

To ask about time, interrogatives using nan, such as nan-ji, nan-yōbi and nan-gatsu nan-nichi are used. The interrogative itsu (when) is also used to ask when something will happen or happened. itsu does not take the particle ni.

⑫ Itsu Nihon e kimashita ka.

······3-gatsu 25-nichi ni kimashita.

When did you come to Japan?

······[I came] on 25th March.

⑬ Itsu Hiroshima e ikimasu ka.

······Raishū ikimasu.

When are you going to Hiroshima?

······[I'm going] next week.

6. ~ yo

The particle yo is placed at the end of a sentence. It is used to emphasise information which the listener does not know, or to show that the speaker is giving his or her judgement or views assertively.

⑭ Kono densha wa Kōshien e ikimasu ka.

······Iie, ikimasen. Tsugi no "futsū" desu yo.

Does this train go to Koshien?

······No, it doesn't. You need the next local train.

⑮ Hokkaidō ni uma ga takusan imasu yo.

There are a lot of horses in Hokkaido, you know. (See Lesson 18.)

⑯ Maria-san, kono aisukuriimu, oishii desu yo.

Maria, this ice cream is very nice, you know. (See Lesson 19.)

7. sō desu ne

The expression sō desu ne is used to express sympathy or agreement with what the speaker has said. It is similar to the expression sō desu ka (see Lesson 2-8), but while sō desu ka is used by a speaker to acknowledge the receipt of some new information, sō desu ne is used to show sympathy or agreement with something the speaker already thought or knew.

⑰ Ashita wa Nichi-yōbi desu ne.

······A, sō desu ne.

It's Sunday tomorrow, isn't it?

······Oh, yes, so it is.

Lesson 6

I. Vocabulary

tabemasu	たべます	eat
nomimasu	のみます	drink
suimasu [tabako o 〜]	すいます [たばこを〜]	smoke [a cigarette]
mimasu	みます	see, look at, watch
kikimasu	ききます	hear, listen
yomimasu	よみます	read
kakimasu	かきます	write, draw, paint
kaimasu	かいます	buy
torimasu	とります	take [a photograph]
[shashin o 〜]	[しゃしんを〜]	
shimasu	します	do, play
aimasu	あいます	meet [a friend]
[tomodachi ni 〜]	[ともだちに〜]	
gohan	ごはん	a meal, cooked rice
asagohan*	あさごはん	breakfast
hirugohan	ひるごはん	lunch
bangohan*	ばんごはん	supper
pan	パン	bread
tamago	たまご	egg
niku	にく	meat
sakana	さかな	fish
yasai	やさい	vegetable
kudamono	くだもの	fruit
mizu	みず	water
ocha	おちゃ	tea, green tea
kōcha	こうちゃ	black tea
gyūnyū (miruku)	ぎゅうにゅう (ミルク)	milk
jūsu	ジュース	juice
biiru	ビール	beer
[o-]sake	[お]さけ	alcohol, Japanese rice wine
tabako	たばこ	tobacco, cigarette

tegami	てがみ	letter
repōto	レポート	report
shashin	しゃしん	photograph
bideo	ビデオ	video [tape], video deck
mise	みせ	shop, store
niwa	にわ	garden
shukudai	しゅくだい	homework （～ o shimasu：do homework）
tenisu	テニス	tennis （～ o shimasu：play tennis）
sakkā	サッカー	soccer, football （～ o shimasu：play soccer）
[o-]hanami	[お]はなみ	cherry-blossom viewing （～ o shimasu：view the cherry blossoms）
nani	なに	what
issho ni	いっしょに	together
chotto	ちょっと	a little while, a little bit
itsumo	いつも	always, usually
tokidoki	ときどき	sometimes
sorekara	それから	after that, and then
ē	ええ	yes
Ii desu ne.	いいですね。	That's good.
Wakarimashita.	わかりました。	I see.

〈Kaiwa〉

Nan desu ka.	なんですか。	Yes? (lit: What is it?)
Ja, mata [ashita].	じゃ、また［あした］。	See you [tomorrow].

....

Mekishiko	メキシコ	Mexico
Ōsaka-depāto	おおさかデパート	a fictitious department store
Tsuru-ya	つるや	a fictitious restaurant
Furansu-ya	フランスや	a fictitious supermarket
Mainichi-ya	まいにちや	a fictitious supermarket

41

II. Translation

Sentence Patterns

1. I [am going to] read a book.
2. I [am going to] buy a newspaper at the station.
3. Shall we go to Kobe together?
4. Let's take a bit of a break.

Example Sentences

1. Do you drink alcohol?
   ······No, I don't.

2. What do you usually have to eat in the morning?
   ······I have bread and eggs.

3. What did you have to eat this morning?
   ······I didn't have anything.

4. What did you do on Saturday?
   ······I studied Japanese, then I watched a film with some friends.

5. Where did you buy that bag?
   ······[I bought it] in Mexico.

6. Shall we play tennis tomorrow?
   ······Yes, that would be great.

7. Let's meet at the station tomorrow at ten o'clock.
   ······OK.

Conversation

Shall we go together?

Sato: Mr. Miller!

Miller: Yes?

Sato: I'm going to see the cherry blossoms tomorrow with some friends. Would you like to come with us, Mr. Miller?

Miller: That sounds good. Where are you going?

Sato: Osaka Castle.

Miller: What time shall we go?

Sato: Let's meet at Osaka Station at ten o'clock.

Miller: OK.

Sato: See you tomorrow, then.

III. Useful Words and Information

TABEMONO   Food

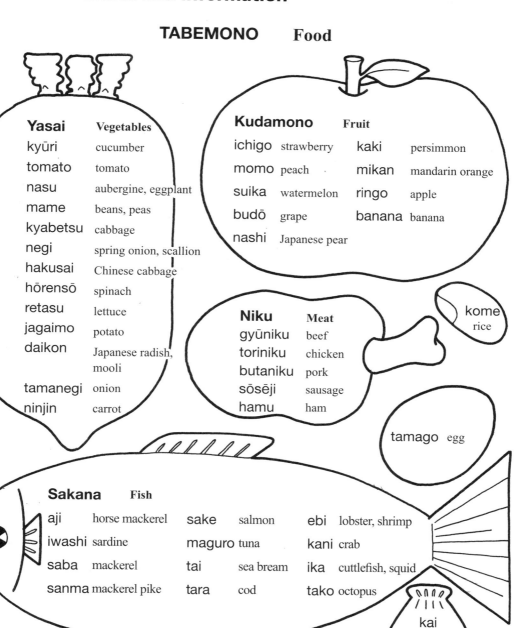

Yasai   Vegetables
kyūri	cucumber
tomato	tomato
nasu	aubergine, eggplant
mame	beans, peas
kyabetsu	cabbage
negi	spring onion, scallion
hakusai	Chinese cabbage
hōrensō	spinach
retasu	lettuce
jagaimo	potato
daikon	Japanese radish, mooli
tamanegi	onion
ninjin	carrot

Kudamono   Fruit
ichigo	strawberry	kaki	persimmon
momo	peach	mikan	mandarin orange
suika	watermelon	ringo	apple
budō	grape	banana	banana
nashi	Japanese pear		

Niku   Meat
gyūniku	beef
toriniku	chicken
butaniku	pork
sōsēji	sausage
hamu	ham

kome rice

tamago egg

Sakana   Fish
aji	horse mackerel	sake	salmon	ebi	lobster, shrimp
iwashi	sardine	maguro	tuna	kani	crab
saba	mackerel	tai	sea bream	ika	cuttlefish, squid
sanma	mackerel pike	tara	cod	tako	octopus

kai shellfish

 Japan depends on imports for more than half of its food. Its food self-sufficiency rates are as follows: cereals 59%, vegetables 81%, fruit 38%, meat 56%, and seafood 60% (2010, Ministry of Agriculture, Forestry, and Fisheries). The self-sufficiency rate of rice (the country's staple food) is 100%.

IV. Grammar Notes

1. N o V (transitive)

The particle o is used to indicate the direct object of a transitive verb.

   ①   Jūsu o nomimasu.   I drink juice.

2. N o shimasu

A fairly wide range of nouns are used as the objects of the verb shimasu, which means that the action denoted by the noun is performed. Some examples are shown below.

1) Play sports or games

       sakkā o shimasu   play soccer   toranpu o shimasu   play cards

2) Hold gatherings or events

       pātii o shimasu   give a party   kaigi o shimasu   hold a meeting

3) Do something

       shukudai o shimasu   do homework   shigoto o shimasu   work

       denwa o shimasu   call, phone

3. Nani o shimasu ka

This is a question to ask about someone's actions.

   ②   Getsu-yōbi nani o shimasu ka.   What are you doing on Monday?

        ······Kyōto e ikimasu.   ······I'm going to Kyoto.

   ③   Kinō nani o shimashita ka.   What did you do yesterday?

        ······Sakkā o shimashita.   ······I played soccer.

4. nan and nani

Both nan and nani mean 'what'.

Nan is used in the following cases:

1) When it precedes a word whose first sound is in the ta-, da- or na-row.

   ④   Sore wa nan <u>d</u>esu ka.   What's that?

   ⑤   Nan <u>no</u> hon desu ka.   What's that book about?

   ⑥   Neru mae ni, nan <u>to</u> iimasu ka.

       What do you say before going to bed? (See Lesson 21.)

   ⑦   Nan <u>de</u> Tōkyō e ikimasu ka.   How are you getting to Tokyo?

[Note] Nan de is used for asking 'Why?' as well as 'How?' Nani de can be used when the speaker wants to make it clear that he or she is asking 'How?'

   ⑧   Nani de Tōkyō e ikimasu ka.   How are you getting to Tokyo?

        ······Shinkansen de ikimasu.   ······I'm going on the Shinkansen.

2) When using it with a counter suffix.

⑨　Terēza-chan wa nan-sai desu ka.　　How old is Teresa?

Nani is used in all other cases apart from 1) and 2).

⑩　Nani o kaimasu ka.　　What are you going to buy?

5. | N (place) de V |

When added after a noun denoting a place, the particle de indicates the occurrence of an action in that place.

⑪　Eki de shinbun o kaimasu.　　I'm going to buy a paper at the station.

6. | V-masen ka |

This expression is used when the speaker wants to invite someone to do something.

⑫　Issho ni Kyōto e ikimasen ka.　　Would you like to come to Kyoto with us?
　　⋯⋯Ē, ii desu ne.　　⋯⋯Yes, that's a nice idea.

7. | V-mashō |

This expression is used when a speaker is positively inviting the listener to do something with the speaker. It is also used when responding positively to an invitation.

⑬　Chotto yasumimashō.　　Let's take a break.
⑭　Issho ni hirugohan o tabemasen ka.　　Shall we have lunch together?
　　⋯⋯Ē, tabemashō.　　⋯⋯Yes, let's do that.

[Note] V-masen ka and V-mashō are both used to invite someone to do something, but V-masen ka shows that the speaker is giving more consideration to what the listener might want than V-mashō.

8. | ～ ka |

Ka indicates that the listener has received and accepted some new information. It is used in the same way as the ka in sō desu ka (see Lesson 2-8).

⑮　Nichi-yōbi Kyōto e ikimashita.　　I went to Kyoto on Sunday.
　　⋯⋯Kyōto desu ka. Ii desu ne.　　⋯⋯Kyoto, eh? Great!

Lesson 7

I. Vocabulary

kirimasu	きります	cut, slice
okurimasu	おくります	send
agemasu	あげます	give
moraimasu	もらいます	receive
kashimasu	かします	lend
karimasu	かります	borrow
oshiemasu	おしえます	teach
naraimasu	ならいます	learn
kakemasu [denwa o ～]	かけます［でんわを～］	make [a telephone call]
te	て	hand, arm
hashi	はし	chopsticks
supūn	スプーン	spoon
naifu	ナイフ	knife
fōku	フォーク	fork
hasami	はさみ	scissors
pasokon	パソコン	personal computer
kētai	ケータイ	mobile phone, cell phone
mēru	メール	e-mail
nengajō	ねんがじょう	New Year's greeting card
panchi	パンチ	punch
hotchikisu	ホッチキス	stapler
serotēpu	セロテープ	Sellotape, Scotch tape, clear adhesive tape
keshigomu	けしゴム	rubber, eraser
kami	かみ	paper
hana	はな	flower, blossom
shatsu	シャツ	shirt
purezento	プレゼント	present, gift
nimotsu	にもつ	luggage, baggage, parcel
okane	おかね	money
kippu	きっぷ	ticket
Kurisumasu	クリスマス	Christmas

chichi	ちち	(my) father
haha	はは	(my) mother
otōsan*	おとうさん	(someone else's) father (also used to address one's own father)
okāsan	おかあさん	(someone else's) mother (also used to address one's own mother)
mō	もう	already
mada	まだ	not yet
korekara	これから	from now on, soon

〈Renshū C〉

[〜,] suteki desu ne.	[〜、] すてきですね。	What a nice [〜]!

〈Kaiwa〉

Irasshai.	いらっしゃい。	How nice of you to come. (lit. Welcome.)
Dōzo o-agari kudasai.	どうぞ おあがり ください。	Do come in.
Shitsurei-shimasu.	しつれいします。	May I? (lit. I commit an incivility.)
[〜wa] ikaga desu ka.	[〜は] いかがですか。	Won't you have [〜]?/Would you like to have [〜]? (used when offering something)
Itadakimasu.	いただきます。	Thank you./I accept. (said before starting to eat or drink)
Gochisōsama [deshita].*	ごちそうさま[でした]。	That was delicious. (said after eating or drinking)

7

47

Supein	スペイン	Spain

Other notes:

e-to (go)
Movie = Eiga
kasa = letter
yoko = -steki = steak
trip
hands = te

shoyu = Soy
sauce

Omiyage = souvenir

hashii de
Nande = how/what
Hambaga
pasta

ka do = card

II. Translation

Sentence Patterns

1. I [am going to] watch a film on my PC.
2. I [am going to] give some flowers to Ms. Kimura.
3. Karina gave me some chocolates (lit. I received some chocolates from Karina.)
4. I've already sent an e-mail.

Example Sentences

1. Did you study Japanese on the TV?
   ······No, I studied it on the radio.

2. Do you write your reports in Japanese?
   ······No, I write them in English.

3. What's 'Goodbye' in Japanese?
   ······It's 'Sayonara'.

4. Who do you write New Year's cards to?
   ······I write them to my teachers and friends.

5. What's that?
   ······It's a personal organiser. Mr. Yamada gave it to me.

6. Have you bought the tickets for the bullet train yet?
   ······Yes, I have [already bought them].

7. Have you had lunch yet?
   ······No, not yet. I'm just about to.

Conversation

Welcome

Ichiro Yamada:	Yes?
Jose Santos:	It's Jose Santos.

....

Ichiro Yamada:	Hello. (lit: Welcome.) Please come in.
Jose Santos:	Thank you.

....

Tomoko Yamada:	Would you like some coffee?
Maria Santos:	Yes, please.

....

Tomoko Yamada:	Here you are.
Maria Santos:	Thank you.
	This is a lovely spoon, isn't it?
Tomoko Yamada:	Yes, I was given it by someone at work.
	It's a souvenir from Mexico.

7

III. Useful Words and Information

KAZOKU Family

WATASHI NO KAZOKU My family

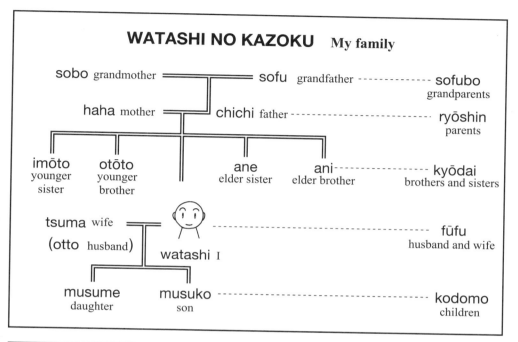

TANAKA-SAN NO KAZOKU Mr. (Ms.) Tanaka's family

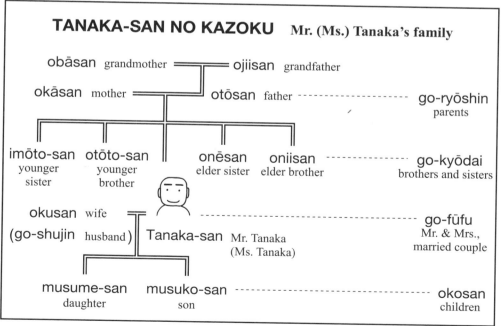

IV. Grammar Notes

1. | N (tool/means) **de** V |

The particle de indicates a method or means used for an action.

①   Hashi de tabemasu.   I eat with chopsticks.

②   Nihon-go de repōto o kakimasu.   I'm going to write the report in Japanese.

2. | 'Word/Sentence' **wa -go de nan desu ka** |

This question is used to ask how to say a word or sentence in another language.

③   "Arigatō" wa Eigo de nan desu ka.   What's 'Arigato' in English?
       ······ "Thank you" desu.   ······It's 'thank you'.

④   "Thank you" wa Nihon-go de nan desu ka.   What's 'thank you' in Japanese?
       ······"Arigatō" desu.   ······It's 'Arigato'.

3. | N_1 (person) **ni** N_2 **o agemasu**, etc. |

Verbs like agemasu, kashimasu and oshiemasu indicate imparting things or information, so they must be used with a noun saying to whom those things or information are imparted. The particle ni is used to denote the recipient.

⑤   [Watashi wa] Kimura-san ni hana o agemashita.   I gave Ms. Kimura some flowers.

⑥   [Watashi wa] Ii-san ni hon o kashimashita.   I lent Ms. Lee a book.

⑦   [Watashi wa] Yamada-san ni Eigo o oshiemasu.   I teach Mr. Yamada English.

4. | N_1 (person) **ni** N_2 **o moraimasu**, etc. |

Verbs like moraimasu, karimasu and naraimasu indicate receiving things or information, so they are used with a noun indicating the person from whom those things or information are received. The particle ni is used to denote that person.

⑧   [Watashi wa] Yamada-san ni hana o moraimashita.
     I received some flowers from Mr. Yamada.

⑨   [Watashi wa] Karina-san ni CD o karimashita.
     I borrowed a CD from Karina.

⑩   [Watashi wa] Wan-san ni Chūgoku-go o naraimasu.
     I'm learning Chinese from Mr. Wang.

[Note] Kara can be used instead of ni in this sentence pattern. Kara is always used when receiving something from an organisation such as a company or school rather than a person.

⑪   [Watashi wa] Yamada-san kara hana o moraimashita.
     I received some flowers from Mr. Yamada.

⑫ Ginkō kara okane o karimashita.
    I borrowed some money from the bank.

5. | Mō V-mashita |

Mō means 'already' and is used with V-mashita. In this case, V-mashita means that the action has been completed.

The answer to the question mō V-mashita ka as to whether an action has been completed or not is hai, mō V-mashita if in the affirmative (i.e. the action has been completed) and iie, V-te imasen (see Lesson 31) or iie, mada desu if in the negative (i.e. the action has not been completed). Iie, V-masendeshita is not used in this case, since this means that something was not done in the past, rather than that something has not been completed in the present.

⑬ Mō nimotsu o okurimashita ka.   Have you sent the baggage yet?
    ·····Hai, [mō] okurimashita.   ·····Yes, I have [sent it].
    ·····Iie, mada okutte imasen.   ·····No, I haven't sent it yet.
                                                       (See Lesson 31.)
    ·····Iie, mada desu.   ·····No, not yet.

6. Omission of particles

Particles are often omitted in informal speech when the relationships between the parts of speech before and after them are obvious.

⑭ Kono supūn [wa], suteki desu ne.   This is a lovely spoon, isn't it?
⑮ Kōhii [o], mō ippai ikaga desu ka.
    Would you like another cup of coffee? (See Lesson 8.)

7

Lesson 8

I. Vocabulary

Kakoi (handwritten)

~~hansamu~~[na]	ハンサム［な］	handsome
kirei[na]	きれい［な］	beautiful, clean
shizuka[na]	しずか［な］	quiet
nigiyaka[na]	にぎやか［な］	lively *urusai=noisy* (handwritten)
yūmei[na]	ゆうめい［な］	famous
shinsetsu[na]	しんせつ［な］	helpful, kind, considerate (not used about one's own family members)
genki[na]	げんき［な］	healthy, energetic, cheerful
hima[na]	ひま［な］	free (time)
benri[na]	べんり［な］	convenient
suteki[na]	すてき［な］	fine, nice, wonderful
ōkii	おおきい	big, large
chiisai*	ちいさい	small, little
atarashii	あたらしい	new, fresh
furui	ふるい	old (not used to describe a person's age)
ii (yoi)	いい（よい）	good
warui*	わるい	bad
atsui	あつい	hot
samui	さむい	cold (referring to temperature)
tsumetai	つめたい	cold (referring to touch)
muzukashii	むずかしい	difficult
yasashii	やさしい	easy
takai	たかい	expensive, tall, high
yasui	やすい	inexpensive, cheap
hikui*	ひくい	low
omoshiroi	おもしろい	interesting
oishii	おいしい	delicious, tasty
isogashii	いそがしい	busy
tanoshii	たのしい	enjoyable
shiroi	しろい	white
kuroi	くろい	black
akai	あかい	red
aoi	あおい	blue
sakura	さくら	cherry (blossom)
yama	やま	mountain
machi	まち	town, city
tabemono	たべもの	food

8

tokoro	ところ	place
ryō	りょう	dormitory
resutoran	レストラン	restaurant
seikatsu	せいかつ	life
[o-]shigoto	[お]しごと	work, business one's job, work
dō	どう	how
donna ～	どんな ～	what kind of ～
totemo	とても	very
amari	あまり	not so (used with negatives)
soshite	そして	and (used to connect sentences)
～ ga, ～	～が、～	～, but ～

(handwritten: amari = not very amari)

〈Renshū C〉

O-genki desu ka.	おげんきですか。	How are you?
Sō desu ne.	そうですね。	Well let me see. (pausing)

(handwritten: restroom)

〈Kaiwa〉

[～,] mō ippai ikaga desu ka.	[～、] もう いっぱい いかがですか。	Won't you have another cup of [～]?
[Iie,] kekkō desu.	[いいえ、] けっこうです。	No, thank you.
Mō ～ desu [ne].	もう ～です[ね]。	It's already ～[, isn't it?]
Sorosoro shitsurei-shimasu.	そろそろ しつれい します。	It's time I was going.
Iie.	いいえ。	Not at all.
Mata irasshatte kudasai.	また いらっしゃって ください。	Please come again.

(handwritten: yaku = thousand; totemo = very; ja arimasen; ku nai desu)

....

Shanhai	シャンハイ	Shanghai (上海)
Kinkakuji	きんかくじ	Kinkakuji Temple (the Golden Pavilion)
Nara-kōen	ならこうえん	Nara Park
Fujisan	ふじさん	Mt. Fuji, the highest mountain in Japan
"Shichi-nin no samurai"	「しちにんの さむらい」	'The Seven Samurai', a classic movie by Akira Kurosawa

(handwritten: biru = building; wa item wa adjitive (desu ka))

8

53

1. Cherry blossoms are beautiful.
2. Mt. Fuji is high.
3. Cherry blossoms are beautiful flowers.
4. Mt. Fuji is a high mountain.

Example Sentences
1. Is Osaka lively?
    ······Yes, it is [lively].

2. Is Sakura University well-known?
    ······No, it's not [well-known].

3. Is it cold in Beijing at the moment?
    ······Yes, it's very cold.

    Is it cold in Shanghai too?
    ······No, it isn't [very cold].

4. How's the university dormitory?
    ······It's old, but it's convenient.

5. I went to Mr. Matsumoto's house yesterday.
    ······What's his house like?
    It's a beautiful house, and it's [a] big [house].

6. I watched an interesting film yesterday.
    ······What did you watch?
    'The Seven Samurai'.

Conversation

It's time we were going

Ichiro Yamada:	Maria, how do you find living in Japan?
Maria Santos:	Every day is great fun.
Ichiro Yamada:	Really? Mr. Santos, how's your work going?
Jose Santos:	Well, it's busy, but it's interesting.

···

Tomoko Yamada:	Would you like another cup of coffee?
Maria Santos:	No, I'm fine, thank you.

···

Jose Santos:	Oh, it's already six o'clock, isn't it? It's time we were going.
Ichiro Yamada:	Really?
Maria Santos:	Thank you very much for today.
Tomoko Yamada:	Not at all. Please come again.

8

54

III. Useful Words and Information

IRO · AJI   Colours and Tastes

Iro Colours

noun		adjective	noun		adjective
shiro	white	shiroi	kiiro	yellow	kiiroi
kuro	black	kuroi	chairo	brown	chairoi
aka	red	akai	pinku	pink	—
ao	blue	aoi	orenji	orange	—
midori	green	—	gurē	gray	—
murasaki	purple	—	bēju	beige	—

Aji Tastes

amai sweet
karai hot (spicy)
nigai bitter
shiokarai salty

suppai sour
koi strong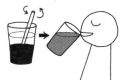
usui weak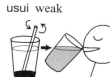

 Haru·Natsu·Aki·Fuyu Spring, Summer, Autumn, Winter

The four seasons are clearly defined in Japan. Spring is from March to May, summer from June to August, autumn from September to November, and winter from December to February. The average temperature varies from place to place, but the pattern of change is almost the same (see graph). August is the hottest month, and January or February are the coldest. As a result of these temperature changes, Japanese people feel that spring is warm, summer hot, autumn cool, and winter cold.

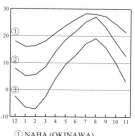

① NAHA (OKINAWA)
② TOKYO
③ ABASHIRI (HOKKAIDO)

IV. Grammar Notes

1. Adjectives

Adjectives are used as predicates, and in sentences like N wa adj desu they indicate the state of a noun or are used to modify a noun. They are divided into one of two groups, i-adjectives and na-adjectives, depending on how they inflect.

2.

> N wa na-adj [n̪á] desu
> N wa i-adj (～ i) desu

Adjective sentences that are non-past and affirmative end in desu, which shows politeness toward the listener. Both types of adjective are attached to the front of desu, but na-adjectives drop their na, while i-adjectives retain their (～i).

① Watto-sensei wa shinsetsu desu.　　Mr. Watt is kind.

② Fujisan wa takai desu.　　Mt. Fuji is high.

1) na-adj [n̪á] ja (dewa) arimasen

The non-past negative of a na-adj is formed by dropping the na and attaching ja (dewa) arimasen to it.

③ Asoko wa shizuka ja (dewa) arimasen.　　It's not quiet there.

2) i-adj (～i) desu → ～kunai desu

The non-past negative of an i-adjective is formed by dropping the final i and attaching kunai desu to it.

④ Kono hon wa omoshirokunai desu.　　This book is not interesting.

[Note] The negative of ii desu is yokunai desu.

3) Adjectival Inflections

	na-adjectives	i-adjectives
Non-past affirmative	shinsetsu desu	takai desu
Non-past negative	shinsetsu ja (dewa) arimasen	takakunai desu

4) Questions using adjective sentences are formed in the same way as those using noun sentences (see Lesson 1) and verb sentences (see Lesson 4). To answer such a question, the adjective is repeated. Expressions such as sō desu or chigaimasu cannot be used.

⑤ Pekin wa samui desu ka.　　Is it cold in Beijing?
　　······Hai, samui desu.　　······Yes, it is [cold].

⑥ Nara-kōen wa nigiyaka desu ka.　　Is Nara Park busy?
　　······Iie, nigiyaka ja arimasen.　　······No, it isn't [busy].

3.

> na-adj na N
> i-adj (～ i) N

When an adjective is used to modify a noun, it is placed in front of the noun. na-adjectives keep their na in this case.

⑦ Watto-sensei wa shinsetsuna sensei desu. Mr. Watt is a considerate teacher.

⑧ Fujisan wa takai yama desu.   Mt. Fuji is a high mountain.

4. ~ ga, ~

Ga connects two statements in an antithetical relationship. When these are adjective clauses with the same subject, if the initial clause remarks on the subject positively, the subsequent clause will remark on it negatively, and vice versa.

⑨ Nihon no tabemono wa oishii desu ga, takai desu.
   Japanese food is delicious, but it is expensive.

5. totemo/amari

Totemo and amari are both adverbs of degree, and both come before the adjectives they modify. Totemo is used in affirmative sentences, and means 'very'. Amari, used with a negative, means 'not very'.

⑩ Pekin wa totemo samui desu.   Beijing is very cold.

⑪ Kore wa totemo yūmeina eiga desu.   This is a very famous movie.

⑫ Shanhai wa amari samukunai desu.   Shanghai is not very cold.

⑬ Sakura-daigaku wa amari yūmeina daigaku ja arimasen.
   Sakura University is not a very well-known university.

6. N wa dō desu ka

The question N wa dō desu ka is used to inquire about the listener's impression, opinion or feelings about a thing, place, person, etc. that he or she has experienced, visited or met.

⑭ Nihon no seikatsu wa dō desu ka.   How do you find life in Japan?
   ······Tanoshii desu.   ······It's fun.

7. N₁ wa donna N₂ desu ka

Donna modifies a noun and is an interrogative used for inquiring about the state or nature of a person, thing, etc.

⑮ Nara wa donna machi desu ka.   What sort of town is Nara?
   ······Furui machi desu.   ······It's an old town.

8. sō desu ne

The use of the expression sō desu ne to express agreement or sympathy was explained in Lesson 5. The sō desu ne that appears in the Conversation of this lesson shows that the speaker is thinking, as in ⑯ below.

⑯ O-shigoto wa dō desu ka.   How's your work going?
   ······Sō desu ne. Isogashii desu ga, omoshiroi desu.
   ······Well, it's busy, but it's interesting.

8

Lesson 9

I. Vocabulary

wakarimasu	わかります	understand
arimasu	あります	have
suki[na]	すき[な]	like
kirai[na]	きらい[な]	dislike
jōzu[na]	じょうず[な]	good at
heta[na]	へた[な]	poor at
nomimono	のみもの	drinks
ryōri	りょうり	dish (cooked food), cooking (〜 o shimasu : cook)
supōtsu	スポーツ	sport (〜 o shimasu : play sports)
yakyū	やきゅう	baseball (〜 o shimasu : play baseball)
dansu	ダンス	dance (〜 o shimasu : dance)
ryokō	りょこう	trip, tour (〜 [o] -shimasu : travel, make a trip)
ongaku	おんがく	music
uta	うた	song
kurashikku	クラシック	classical music
jazu	ジャズ	jazz
konsāto	コンサート	concert
karaoke	カラオケ	karaoke
kabuki	かぶき	Kabuki (traditional Japanese musical drama)
e	え	picture, drawing
ji*	じ	letter, character
kanji	かんじ	Chinese character
hiragana	ひらがな	hiragana script
katakana	かたかな	katakana script
rōmaji*	ローマじ	the Roman alphabet
komakai okane	こまかい おかね	small change
chiketto	チケット	ticket
jikan	じかん	time
yōji	ようじ	something to do, errand
yakusoku	やくそく	appointment, promise (〜 [o] -shimasu : promise)

arubaito	アルバイト	side job (〜 o shimasu：work part-time)
go-shujin	ごしゅじん	(someone else's) husband
otto/shujin	おっと／しゅじん	(my) husband
okusan	おくさん	(someone else's) wife
tsuma/kanai	つま／かない	(my) wife
kodomo	こども	child
yoku	よく	well, much
daitai	だいたい	mostly, roughly
takusan	たくさん	many, much
sukoshi	すこし	a little, a few
zenzen	ぜんぜん	not at all (used with negatives)
hayaku	はやく	early, quickly, fast
〜 kara	〜から	because 〜
dōshite	どうして	why

〈Renshū C〉

Kashite kudasai.	かして ください。	Please lend (it to me).
Ii desu yo.	いいですよ。	Sure./Certainly.
zannen desu [ga]	ざんねんです［が］	I'm sorry [, but], unfortunately

〈Kaiwa〉

ā	ああ	oh
Issho ni ikaga desu ka.	いっしょに いかがですか。	Won't you join me (us)?
[〜 wa] chotto......	［〜は］ちょっと……。	[〜] is a bit difficult. (a euphemism used when declining an invitation)
Dame desu ka.	だめですか。	So you can't (come)?
Mata kondo onegai-shimasu.	また こんど おねがいします。	Please ask me again some other time. (used when refusing an invitation indirectly, considering someone's feelings)

9

II. Translation

Sentence Patterns

1. I like Italian food.
2. I can understand a bit of Japanese.
3. It's my son's (daughter's) birthday today, so I'm going home early.

Example Sentences

1. Do you like alcohol?
   ......No, I don't [like it].

2. What sports do you like?
   ......I like soccer.

3. Is Karina good at painting?
   ......Yes, she's very good.

4. Do you understand Indonesian, Ms. Tanaka?
   ......No, not at all.

5. Do you have any small change?
   ......No, I don't.

6. Do you read the newspaper every morning?
   ......No, I don't; I don't have time.

7. Why did you go home early yesterday?
   ......Because there was something I had to do.

Conversation

It's a pity......

Kimura: Yes?

Miller: Is that Ms. Kimura? This is Mike Miller.

Kimura: Oh, Mr. Miller. Good evening. Are you well?

Miller: Yes, I'm fine.
         Umm...... Ms. Kimura, would you like to come to a classical concert with me?

Kimura: That sounds nice. When is it?

Miller: Next week, on Friday evening.

Kimura: Friday?
         Friday evening's not so good for me.

Miller: So you can't come?

Kimura: No, it's a pity, but I've arranged to meet some friends......

Miller: I see.

Kimura: Yes. Please ask me another time.

III. Useful Words and Information

ONGAKU · SUPŌTSU · EIGA Music, Sports and Films

Ongaku Music

poppusu	pop
rokku	rock
jazu	jazz
raten	Latin-American
kurashikku	classical
min'yō	folk
enka	traditional Japanese popular songs
myūjikaru	musical
opera	opera

Eiga Films

SF	science fiction
horā	horror
anime	cartoon
dokyumentarii	documentary
ren'ai	romance
misuterii	mystery
bungei	film based on a classic work
sensō	war
akushon	action
kigeki	comedy

Supōtsu Sports

sofutobōru	softball	yakyū	baseball
sakkā	soccer	takkyū/pinpon	table tennis, ping-pong
ragubii	rugby	sumō	sumo
barēbōru	volleyball	jūdō	judo
basukettobōru	basketball	kendō	Japanese fencing
tenisu	tennis	suiei	swimming
bōringu	bowling		
sukii	skiing		
sukēto	skating		

IV. Grammar Notes

1. | N ga arimasu/wakarimasu
N ga suki desu/kirai desu/jōzu desu/heta desu

The objects of some verbs and adjectives are marked with ga.

① Watashi wa Itaria-ryōri ga suki desu. I like Italian food.

② Watashi wa Nihon-go ga wakarimasu. I understand Japanese.

③ Watashi wa kuruma ga arimasu. I have a car.

2. | donna N

In addition to the responses explained in Lesson 8, a question sentence using donna may be replied to by stating a specific name.

④ Donna supōtsu ga suki desu ka. What sports do you like?
 ······Sakkā ga suki desu. ······I like soccer.

3. | yoku/daitai/takusan/sukoshi/amari/zenzen

These adverbs are placed before verbs to modify them.

	Adverbs of degree		Adverbs of quantity	
Used with an affirmative	yoku	wakarimasu	takusan	arimasu
	daitai	wakarimasu	sukoshi	arimasu
	sukoshi	wakarimasu		
Used with a negative	amari	wakarimasen	amari	arimasen
	zenzen	wakarimasen	zenzen	arimasen

⑤ Eigo ga yoku wakarimasu. I understand English well.

⑥ Eigo ga sukoshi wakarimasu. I understand English a little.

⑦ Eigo ga amari wakarimasen. I don't understand English very well.

⑧ Okane ga takusan arimasu. I have a lot of money.

⑨ Okane ga zenzen arimasen. I don't have any money.

[Note] Sukoshi, zenzen and amari can also modify adjectives.

⑩ Koko wa sukoshi samui desu. It's a little cold here.

⑪ Ano eiga wa zenzen omoshirokunai desu.
That film is not at all interesting.

4. $\sim$ kara, $\sim$

A statement before kara gives the reason for a statement after it.

⑫ Jikan ga arimasen kara, shinbun o yomimasen.

I don't read newspapers because I don't have time.

It is also possible to state something and add the reason after it by adding $\sim$ kara.

⑬ Maiasa shinbun o yomimasu ka.

······Iie, yomimasen. Jikan ga arimasen kara.

Do you read a newspaper every morning?

······No, I don't. I don't have time.

5. dōshite

The interrogative dōshite is used to ask the reason for something. Kara is placed at the end of the reply giving the reason.

⑭ Dōshite asa shinbun o yomimasen ka.

······Jikan ga arimasen kara.

Why don't you read a newspaper in the mornings?

······Because I don't have time.

The question dōshite desu ka is used to ask the reason for something the other person has just said, instead of repeating what they said.

⑮ Kyō wa hayaku kaerimasu.	I'm going home early today.
······Dōshite desu ka.	······Why?
Kodomo no tanjōbi desu kara.	Because it's my son's (daughter's) birthday.

9

Lesson 10

I. Vocabulary

arimasu	あります	exist, be (referring to inanimate things)
imasu	います	exist, be (referring to animate things)
iroiro[na]	いろいろ[な]	various
otoko no hito	おとこの ひと	man
onna no hito	おんなの ひと	woman
otoko no ko	おとこの こ	boy
onna no ko	おんなの こ	girl
inu	いぬ	dog
neko	ねこ	cat
panda	パンダ	panda
zō	ぞう	elephant
ki	き	tree, wood
mono	もの	thing
denchi	でんち	battery
hako	はこ	box
suitchi	スイッチ	switch
reizōko	れいぞうこ	refrigerator
tēburu	テーブル	table
beddo	ベッド	bed
tana	たな	shelf
doa	ドア	door
mado	まど	window
posuto	ポスト	postbox, mailbox
biru	ビル	building
ATM	ATM	cash machine, ATM (Automatic Teller Machine)
konbini	コンビニ	convenience store
kōen	こうえん	park
kissaten	きっさてん	café, coffee shop
-ya	～や	～ shop, ～ store
noriba	のりば	a fixed place to catch taxis, trains, etc.
ken	けん	prefecture

ue	うえ	on, above, over
shita	した	under, below, beneath
mae	まえ	front, before
ushiro	うしろ	back, behind
migi	みぎ	right [side]
hidari	ひだり	left [side]
naka	なか	in, inside
soto*	そと	outside
tonari	となり	next, next door
chikaku	ちかく	near, vicinity
aida	あいだ	between, among
～ ya ～ [nado]	～や ～[など]	～, ～, and so on

〈Kaiwa〉

[Dōmo] sumimasen.	[どうも] すみません。	Thank you.
nanpurā	ナンプラー	nam pla
kōnā	コーナー	corner, section
ichiban shita	いちばん した	the bottom

Tōkyō Dizuniirando	とうきょうディズニーランド	Tokyo Disneyland
Ajia-sutoa	アジアストア	a fictitious supermarket

II. Translation

Sentence Patterns
1. There's a convenience store over there.
2. Ms. Sato's in the lobby.
3. Tokyo Disneyland's in Chiba prefecture.
4. My family's in New York.

Example Sentences
1. Is there a cash machine in this building?
   ······Yes, it's on the second floor.

2. You see that man over there? Who is he?
   ······That's Mr. Matsumoto from IMC.

3. Who's in the garden?
   ······Nobody. There's a cat there.

4. What's in the box?
   ······Some old letters, photographs and other stuff.

5. Where's the post office?
   ······It's near the station, in front of the bank.

6. Where's Mr. Miller?
   ······He's in the meeting room.

Conversation
Do you have any nam pla?

Miller:	Excuse me, where's Asia Store?
Woman:	Asia Store?
	You see that white building over there?
	It's in that building.
Miller:	I see. Thank you.
Woman:	Not at all.

··

Miller:	Excuse me, do you have any nam pla?
Shop Assistant:	Yes.
	There's a Thai food section over there.
	The nam pla's right at the bottom.
Miller:	I see. Thanks.

III. Useful Words and Information

UCHI NO NAKA   Inside the House

① genkan   entrance hall   ⑥ shokudō   dining room

② toire   toilet   ⑦ ima   living room

③ furoba   bathroom   ⑧ shinshitsu   bedroom

④ senmenjo   washroom   ⑨ rōka   hall

⑤ daidokoro   kitchen   ⑩ beranda   balcony

 How to Use a Japanese Bath

① Wash and rinse yourself in the tiled area before getting into the bath.

② Soap and shampoo should never be used in the bath. The bath is for warming yourself and relaxing.

③ When you go out of the bathroom, leave the bath full of hot water and cover it so it stays hot for the next person.

How to Use the Toilet

Japanese-style

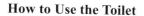

Western-style

IV. Grammar Notes

1. | N ga arimasu/imasu |

Arimasu and imasu indicate the existence of a thing, person, etc. Since a sentence using these simply tells the listener that a thing or person exists, the noun representing that thing or person is marked by ga.

1) Arimasu is used when what is present is inanimate and cannot move by itself, such as plants and objects.

   ①   Konpyūtā ga arimasu.   There's a computer.

   ②   Sakura ga arimasu.   There are cherry trees.

   ③   Kōen ga arimasu.   There's a park.

2) Imasu is used when what is present is animate and can move by itself, like people and animals.

   ④   Otoko no hito ga imasu.   There's a man.

   ⑤   Inu ga imasu.   There's a dog.

2. | Place ni N ga arimasu/imasu |

This sentence form is used to say what or who is in a certain place.

1) The particle ni is used to mark the place where the thing or person is.

   ⑥   Watashi no heya ni tsukue ga arimasu.   There's a desk in my room.

   ⑦   Jimusho ni Mirā-san ga imasu.   Mr. Miller is in the office.

2) The interrogative nani is used when asking what is present, while the interrogative dare is used when asking who is present.

   ⑧   Chika ni nani ga arimasu ka.   What's in the basement?
      ……Resutoran ga arimasu.   ……There's a restaurant.

   ⑨   Uketsuke ni dare ga imasu ka.   Who's at the reception desk?
      ……Kimura-san ga imasu.   ……Ms. Kimura is.

[Note] Remember that the particle used after an interrogative is always ga
(× nani wa   × dare wa).

3. | N wa place ni arimasu/imasu |

This type of sentence takes the noun (the thing that exists) of 2. Place ni N ga arimasu/imasu as its topic and talks about its existence. The noun is positioned at the head of the sentence and is marked with wa. In this case, the noun must be something that both the speaker and the listener are aware of.

   ⑩   Tōkyō Dizuniirando wa Chiba-ken ni arimasu.
      Tokyo Disneyland is in Chiba prefecture.

   ⑪   Mirā-san wa jimusho ni imasu.   Mr. Miller is in the office.

   ⑫   Tōkyō Dizuniirando wa doko ni arimasu ka.   Where's Tokyo Disneyland?

……Chiba-ken ni arimasu.   ……It's in Chiba prefecture.

⑬ Mirā-san wa doko ni imasu ka.   Where's Mr Miller?

    ……Jimusho ni imasu.   ……He's in the office.

[Note] This sentence form can be replaced with N wa place desu (see Lesson 3). Note that the interrogative (doko) or N (Chiba-ken) which comes before desu and represents the place is not marked by ni in this case.

⑭ Tōkyō Dizuniirando wa doko desu ka.   Where's Tokyo Disneyland?

    ……Chiba-ken desu.   ……It's in Chiba prefecture.

4.   N₁ (thing/person/place) **no** N₂ (position)

When the noun N₂ represents a direction or a position, e.g. ue, shita, mae, ushiro, migi, hidari, naka, soto, tonari, chikaku or aida, it shows a positional relationship with N₁.

⑮ Tsukue no ue ni shashin ga arimasu.   There's a photograph on the desk.

⑯ Yūbinkyoku wa ginkō no tonari ni arimasu. The post office is next to the bank.

⑰ Hon-ya wa hana-ya to sūpā no aida ni arimasu.

    The bookshop is between the florist and the supermarket.

[Note] In the same way as with nouns representing place, the location of an action can be indicated by attaching the particle de to these.

⑱ Eki no chikaku de tomodachi ni aimashita. I met a friend near the station.

5.   N₁ **ya** N₂

As explained in Lesson 4, the particle to is used to connect nouns in coordinate relation when enumerating a list of nouns. In contrast to this, the particle ya is used when only a few (two or more) representative items are enumerated. Nado is sometimes put after the last noun to make it clear that the speaker has not mentioned all the nouns that could be on the list.

⑲ Hako no naka ni tegami ya shashin ga arimasu.

    There are some letters, photographs and other things in the box.

⑳ Hako no naka ni tegami ya shashin nado ga arimasu.

    There are some letters, photographs and other things in the box.

6.   Ajia-sutoa desu ka

The following dialogue occurs at the beginning of this Lesson's conversation:

㉑ Sumimasen. Ajia-sutoa wa doko desu ka.

    ……Ajia-sutoa desu ka. (chūryaku) Ano biru no naka desu.

    Excuse me, where is Asia Store?

    ……Asia Store? (sentence omitted) It's in that building.

In actual conversation, people often do not reply immediately to a question they have been asked, but first confirm the main point of the question in this way.

Lesson 11

I. Vocabulary

imasu [kodomo ga 〜]	います［こどもが〜］	have [a child]
imasu [Nihon ni 〜]	います［にほんに〜］	stay, be [in Japan]
kakarimasu	かかります	take, cost (referring to time or money)
yasumimasu	やすみます	take a day off [work]
[kaisha o 〜]	［かいしゃを〜］	
hitotsu	ひとつ	one (used when counting things)
futatsu	ふたつ	two
mittsu	みっつ	three
yottsu	よっつ	four
itsutsu	いつつ	five
muttsu	むっつ	six
nanatsu	ななつ	seven
yattsu	やっつ	eight
kokonotsu	ここのつ	nine
tō	とお	ten
ikutsu	いくつ	how many
hitori	ひとり	one person
futari	ふたり	two people
-nin	－にん	－ people
-dai	－だい	(counter for machines, cars, etc.)
-mai	－まい	(counter for paper, stamps, etc.)
-kai	－かい	－ times
ringo	りんご	apple
mikan	みかん	mandarin orange
sandoitchi	サンドイッチ	sandwich
karē[-raisu]	カレー［ライス］	curry [with rice]
aisukuriimu	アイスクリーム	ice cream
kitte	きって	postage stamp
hagaki	はがき	postcard
fūtō	ふうとう	envelope
ryōshin	りょうしん	parents
kyōdai	きょうだい	brothers and sisters
ani	あに	(my) elder brother

oniisan*	おにいさん	(someone else's) elder brother
ane	あね	(my) elder sister
onēsan*	おねえさん	(someone else's) elder sister
otōto	おとうと	(my) younger brother
otōtosan*	おとうとさん	(someone else's) younger brother
imōto	いもうと	(my) younger sister
imōtosan*	いもうとさん	(someone else's) younger sister
gaikoku	がいこく	foreign country
ryūgakusei	りゅうがくせい	foreign student
kurasu	クラス	class
-jikan	－じかん	－ hour(s)
-shūkan	－しゅうかん	－ week(s)
-kagetsu	－かげつ	－ month(s)
-nen	－ねん	－ year(s)
～ gurai	～ぐらい	about ～
donokurai	どのくらい	how long
zenbu de	ぜんぶで	in total
minna	みんな	all, everything, everyone
～ dake	～だけ	only ～

〈Renshū C〉

Kashikomarimashita.	かしこまりました。	Certainly, (Sir/Madam).

〈Kaiwa〉

Ii [o-]tenki desu ne.	いい [お]てんきですね。	Nice weather, isn't it?
O-dekake desu ka.	おでかけですか。	Are you going out?
Chotto ～ made.	ちょっと ～まで。	I'm just going to ～.
Itterasshai.	いってらっしゃい。	See you later./So long. (lit. Go and come back.)
Itte kimasu.	いって きます。	See you later./So long. (lit. I'm going and coming back.)
funabin	ふなびん	sea mail
kōkūbin (eamēru)	こうくうびん(エアメール)	airmail
Onegai-shimasu.	おねがいします。	Please. (lit. ask for a favour)

....

Ōsutoraria	オーストラリア	Australia

71

11

II. Translation

Sentence Patterns

1. There are seven tables in the meeting room.
2. I'll be (I've been) in Japan for one year.

Example Sentences

1. How many apples did you buy?
   ······ [I bought] four.

2. Five eighty-yen stamps and two postcards, please.
   ······ Certainly. That'll be five hundred yen altogether.

3. Are there any foreign lecturers at Fuji University?
   ······ Yes, there are three. They're all American.

4. How many brothers and sisters do you have?
   ······ Three. (lit:Four including me.) Two elder sisters and one elder brother.

5. How many times a week do you play tennis?
   ······ [I play] about twice.

6. How long have you been studying Spanish, Mr. Tanaka?
   ······ [I've been studying it for] three months.
   Only three months? You're very good at it, aren't you?

7. How long does it take from Osaka to Tokyo on the bullet train?
   ······ [It takes] two and a half hours.

11

Conversation

[I'd like to send] this, please

Janitor:	Lovely weather, isn't it? Are you going out?
Wang:	Yes, just to the post office.
Janitor:	Are you? See you later.
Wang:	See you.

....

Wang:	I'd like to send this to Australia, please.
Post Office Clerk:	Of course. Sea mail, or airmail?
Wang:	How much is airmail?
Post Office Clerk:	[It's] ¥7,600.
Wang:	And sea mail?
Post Office Clerk:	[It's] ¥3,450.
Wang:	How long does it take?
Post Office clerk:	Around seven days by air and two months by sea.
Wang:	All right, I'll send it by sea mail, please.

III. Useful Words and Information

MENYŪ   Menu

teishoku	set meal
ranchi	western-style set meal
tendon	a bowl of rice with fried seafood and vegetables
oyakodon	a bowl of rice with chicken and egg
gyūdon	a bowl of rice with beef
yaki-niku	grilled meat
yasai-itame	sautéed vegetables
tsukemono	pickles
misoshiru	miso soup
onigiri	rice ball

tenpura	fried seafood and vegetables
sushi	vinegared rice with raw fish
udon	Japanese noodles made from wheat flour
soba	Japanese noodles made from buckwheat flour
rāmen	Chinese noodles in soup with meat and vegetables
yaki-soba	Chinese stir-fried noodles with pork and vegetables
okonomiyaki	a type of pancake grilled with meat, vegetables and egg

karē-raisu	curry with rice
hanbāgu	hamburg steak
korokke	croquette
ebi-furai	fried shrimp
furaido-chikin	fried chicken
sarada	salad
sūpu	soup
supagetti	spaghetti
piza	pizza
hanbāgā	hamburger
sandoitchi	sandwich
tōsuto	toast
kōhii	coffee
kōcha	black tea
kokoa	cocoa
jūsu	juice
kōra	cola

11

IV. Grammar Notes

1. How to say numbers

1) The words hitotsu, futatsu,······tō are used to count things up to 10. The numbers themselves are used when counting things from 11 and higher.

2) Counter suffixes

When counting people and things, various different counter suffixes are used depending on what is being counted.

-nin	People, except for one and two. One person is counted hitori, and two people are counted futari. 4-nin is pronounced yonin.
-dai	machines and vehicles
-mai	thin, flat things such as paper, shirts, dishes, and CDs
-kai	frequency, number of times
-fun (-pun)	minutes
-jikan	hours
-nichi	days (This is the same as for dates, but 'one day' is ichi-nichi, not tsuitachi.)
-shūkan	weeks
-kagetsu	months
-nen	years

2. How to use quantifiers

1) Quantifiers (numbers with counter suffixes) are usually put straight after the noun + particle that determines the type of quantifier. However, this is not always the case with length of time.

① Ringo o yottsu kaimashita.　　　　　I bought four apples.

② Gaikokujin no gakusei ga futari imasu.　There are two foreign students.

③ Kuni de 2-kagetsu Nihon-go o benkyō-shimashita.
I studied Japanese for two months in my home country.

2) Asking how many

(1) Ikutsu

The word ikutsu is used when asking how many there are of the items counted by the method explained in 1-1).

④ Mikan o ikutsu kaimashita ka.　　　How many mandarin oranges did you buy?
　　······Yattsu kaimashita.　　　　　······[I bought] eight.

(2) Nan + counter suffix

Nan + counter suffix is used when asking how many there are of things with a counter suffix attached as in 1-2).

⑤ Kono kaisha ni gaikokujin ga nan-nin imasu ka.
······5-nin imasu.

How many foreign people are there in this company?
······ [There are] five.

⑥ Maiban nan-jikan Nihon-go o benkyō-shimasu ka.
······2-jikan benkyō-shimasu.

How many hours do you study Japanese every night?
······[I study for] two hours.

(3) Donokurai

Donokurai is used to ask the length of time something takes.

⑦ Donokurai Nihon-go o benkyō-shimashita ka.
······3-nen benkyō-shimashita.

How long did you study Japanese for?
······[I studied it for] three years.

⑧ Ōsaka kara Tōkyō made donokurai kakarimasu ka.
······Shinkansen de 2-jikan han kakarimasu.

How long does it take from Osaka to Tokyo?
······[It takes] two and a half hours by Shinkansen.

3) 〜 gurai

Gurai is added after quantifiers to mean 'about'.

⑨ Gakkō ni sensei ga 30-nin gurai imasu.

There are about thirty teachers at our school.

⑩ 15-fun gurai kakarimasu.　　　　　　It takes about fifteen minutes.

3. | Quantifier (time period) ni -kai V |

This expression indicates frequency.

⑪ 1-kagetsu ni 2-kai eiga o mimasu.　　I go to see a film about twice a month.

4. | Quantifier dake/N dake |

Dake means 'only'. It is added after quantifiers or nouns to indicate that there is no more or nothing else.

⑫ Pawā-denki ni gaikokujin no shain ga hitori dake imasu.

There is only one foreign employee at Power Electric.

⑬ Yasumi wa nichi-yōbi dake desu.　　Sunday is my only day off.

Lesson 12

I. Vocabulary

kantan[na]	かんたん［な］	easy, simple
chikai	ちかい	near
tōi*	とおい	far
hayai	はやい	fast, early
osoi*	おそい	slow, late
ōi [hito ga 〜]	おおい ［ひとが〜］	many [people], much
sukunai* [hito ga 〜]	すくない ［ひとが〜］	few [people], a little
atatakai	あたたかい	warm
suzushii	すずしい	cool
amai	あまい	sweet
karai	からい	hot (taste), spicy
omoi	おもい	heavy
karui*	かるい	light
ii [kōhii ga 〜]	いい ［コーヒーが〜］	prefer [coffee]
kisetsu	きせつ	season
haru	はる	spring
natsu	なつ	summer
aki	あき	autumn, fall
fuyu	ふゆ	winter
tenki	てんき	weather
ame	あめ	rain, rainy
yuki	ゆき	snow, snowy
kumori	くもり	cloudy
hoteru	ホテル	hotel
kūkō	くうこう	airport
umi	うみ	sea, ocean
sekai	せかい	world
pātii	パーティー	party（〜 o shimasu : give a party）
[o-]matsuri	［お］まつり	festival

sukiyaki*	すきやき	sukiyaki (beef and vegetable hot pot)
sashimi*	さしみ	sashimi (sliced raw fish)
[o-]sushi	[お]すし	sushi (vinegared rice topped with raw fish)
tenpura	てんぷら	tempura (seafood and vegetables deep fried in batter)
butaniku*	ぶたにく	pork
toriniku	とりにく	chicken
gyūniku	ぎゅうにく	beef
remon	レモン	lemon
ikebana	いけばな	flower arrangement (〜 o shimasu : practise flower arrangement)
momiji	もみじ	maple, red leaves of autumn
dochira	どちら	which one (of two things)
dochira mo	どちらも	both
ichiban	いちばん	the most
zutto	ずっと	by far
hajimete	はじめて	for the first time

〈Kaiwa〉

Tadaima.	ただいま。	I'm home.
Okaerinasai.	おかえりなさい。	Welcome home.
Wā, sugoi hito desu ne.	わあ、すごい ひとですね。	Wow! Look at all those people!
Tsukaremashita.	つかれました。	I'm tired.

Gion-matsuri	ぎおんまつり	the Gion Festival (the most famous festival in Kyoto)
Honkon	ホンコン	Hong Kong (香港)
Shingapōru	シンガポール	Singapore
ABC-sutoa	ABC ストア	a fictitious supermarket
Japan	ジャパン	a fictitious supermarket

12

II. Translation

Sentence Patterns

1. It was rainy yesterday.
2. It was cold yesterday.
3. Hokkaido is bigger than Kyushu.
4. Summer is my favourite season.

Example Sentences

1. Was Kyoto quiet?
   ······No, it wasn't [quiet].

2. Did you enjoy your trip?
   ······Yes, I did [enjoy it].

   Did you have nice weather?
   ······No, it wasn't very good.

3. How was last night's party?
   ······It was very lively. I met a lot of different people.

4. Is New York colder than Osaka?
   ······Yes, it's much colder.

5. Which takes less time to the airport; the train, or the bus?
   ······The train's quicker.

6. Which do you prefer, the sea or the mountains?
   ······I like them both.

7. Which Japanese dish do you like best?
   ······I like tempura best.

12

Conversation

How was the Gion Festival?

Miller: I'm back!

Janitor: Welcome back.

Miller: Here's a souvenir from Kyoto.

Janitor: Thank you very much.
           How was the Gion Festival?

Miller: It was interesting.
          It was very lively.

Janitor: That's because the Gion Festival is the most famous of Kyoto's festivals.

Miller: Oh, is it?
          I took a lot of photographs. Take a look.

Janitor: Wow! Look at all those people!

Miller: Yes, it was a bit tiring.

III. Useful Words and Information

MATSURI TO MEISHO   Festivals and Places of Note

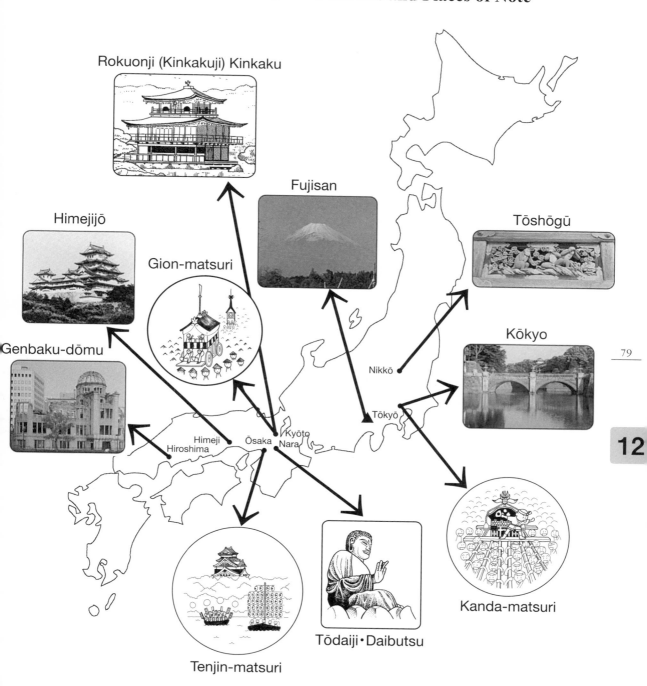

Rokuonji (Kinkakuji) Kinkaku

Fujisan

Tōshōgū

Himejijō

Gion-matsuri

Kōkyo

Genbaku-dōmu

Nikkō

Tōkyō

Himeji
Hiroshima

Ōsaka

Kyōto
Nara

Tenjin-matsuri

Tōdaiji・Daibutsu

Kanda-matsuri

IV. Grammar Notes

1. Tense and affirmative/negative forms of noun sentences and na-adjective sentences

	Non-past (present/future)		Past	
Affirmative	N na-adj	ame shizuka } desu	N na-adj	ame shizuka } deshita
Negative	N na-adj	ame shizuka } ja arimasen (dewa)	N na-adj	ame shizuka } ja arimasendeshita (dewa)

① Kinō wa ame deshita.　　　It was rainy yesterday.

② Kinō no shiken wa kantan ja arimasendeshita.
　Yesterday's exam wasn't easy.

2. Tense and affirmative/negative forms of i-adjective sentences

	Non-past (present/future)	Past
Affirmative	atsui desu	atsukatta desu
Negative	atsukunai desu	atsukunakatta desu

③ Kinō wa atsukatta desu.　　　It was hot yesterday.

④ Kinō no pātii wa amari tanoshikunakatta desu.
　I didn't enjoy yesterday's party very much.

3. N₁ wa N₂ yori adj desu

This sentence pattern describes the quality and/or state of N₁ in comparison with N₂.

⑤ Kono kuruma wa ano kuruma yori ōkii desu.　This car's bigger than that one.

4. N₁ to N₂ to dochira ga adj desu ka
······N₁/N₂ no hō ga adj desu

The interrogative dochira is used when comparing any two items.

⑥ Sakkā to yakyū to dochira ga omoshiroi desu ka.
　······Sakkā no hō ga omoshiroi desu.
　Which [do you think] is more interesting, soccer or baseball?
　······[I think] soccer's more interesting.

⑦ Mirā-san to Santosu-san to dochira ga tenisu ga jōzu desu ka.
　Who's better at tennis, Mr. Miller or Mr. Santos?

⑧ Hokkaidō to Ōsaka to dochira ga suzushii desu ka.
　Which is cooler, Hokkaido or Osaka?

⑨ Haru to aki to dochira ga suki desu ka.
　Which do you prefer, spring or autumn?

5.

$$N_1 \text{ [no naka] de } \begin{Bmatrix} \text{nani} \\ \text{doko} \\ \text{dare} \\ \text{itsu} \end{Bmatrix} \text{ga ichiban adj desu ka}$$

······N₂ **ga ichiban** adj **desu**

De indicates a range. This question pattern is used to ask the listener to choose, from a group or category denoted by N₁, a thing, place, person, time, etc. that exhibits to the highest degree the state or quality described by the adjective. The interrogative used is determined by the kind of category from which the choice is to be made.

⑩ Nihon-ryōri [no naka] de nani ga ichiban oishii desu ka.

······Tenpura ga ichiban oishii desu.

Which of all the Japanese dishes is the most delicious?

······Tempura is [the most delicious].

⑪ Yōroppa de doko ga ichiban yokatta desu ka.

······Suisu ga ichiban yokatta desu.

What was your favorite place in Europe?

······Switzerland was [the best].

⑫ Kazoku de dare ga ichiban se ga takai desu ka.

······Otōto ga ichiban se ga takai desu.

Who is the tallest in your family?

······My younger brother is [the tallest]. (See Lesson 16.)

⑬ 1-nen de itsu ga ichiban samui desu ka.　What's the coldest time of the year?

······2-gatsu ga ichiban samui desu.　······February is [the coldest].

[Note] The particle ga is attached to the interrogative even in an interrogative sentence asking about the subject of an adjective sentence (see Lesson 10).

6. | Adj no | (**no substituting for a noun**)

Lesson 2 explained the use of no in the form N₁ no to substitute for a noun mentioned previously. The no in the phrase atsui no presented in the present lesson's example sentences substitutes for a noun in a similar way, in the form adj no.

⑭ Karina-san no kaban wa dore desu ka.　Which is Karina's bag?

······Ano akakute, ōkii no desu.　······That big red one.

Lesson 13

I. Vocabulary

asobimasu	あそびます	enjoy oneself, play
oyogimasu	およぎます	swim
mukaemasu	むかえます	go to meet, welcome
tsukaremasu	つかれます	get tired (when expressing the condition of being tired, tsukaremashita is used)
kekkon-shimasu	けっこんします	marry, get married
kaimono-shimasu	かいものします	do shopping
shokuji-shimasu	しょくじします	have a meal, dine
sanpo-shimasu [kōen o 〜]	さんぽします [こうえんを〜]	take a walk [in a park]
taihen[na]	たいへん[な]	hard, tough, severe, awful
hoshii	ほしい	want (something)
hiroi	ひろい	wide, spacious
semai	せまい	narrow, small (room, etc.)
pūru	プール	swimming pool
kawa	かわ	river
bijutsu	びじゅつ	fine arts
tsuri	つり	fishing (〜 o shimasu：fish, angle)
sukii	スキー	skiing (〜 o shimasu：ski)
shūmatsu	しゅうまつ	weekend
[o-]shōgatsu	[お]しょうがつ	New Year's Day
〜 goro	〜ごろ	about 〜 (time)
nanika	なにか	something
dokoka	どこか	somewhere, some place

〈Renshū C〉

nodo ga kawakimasu	のどが かわきます	get thirsty (when expressing the condition of being thirsty, nodo ga kawakimashita is used)
onaka ga sukimasu	おなかが すきます	get hungry (when expressing the condition of being hungry, onaka ga sukimashita is used)
Sō shimashō.	そう しましょう。	Let's do that. (used when agreeing with someone's suggestion)

〈Kaiwa〉

Go-chūmon wa?	ごちゅうもんは？	May I take your order?
teishoku	ていしょく	set meal, table d´hôte
gyūdon	ぎゅうどん	bowl of rice topped with beef
[Shōshō] o-machi kudasai.	[しょうしょう] おまち ください。	Please wait [a moment].
～ de gozaimasu.	～で ございます。	(polite equivalent of desu)
betsubetsu ni	べつべつに	separately

....

Akikkusu	アキックス	a fictitious company
Ohayō-terebi	おはようテレビ	a fictitious TV programme

13

II. Translation

Sentence Patterns

1. I want a car.
2. I want to eat some sushi.
3. I'm going to France to study cooking.

Example Sentences

1. What do you want most right now?
   ······[I want] a new mobile phone.

2. Where do you want to go for your summer holiday?
   ······[I want to go to] Okinawa.

3. I feel tired today, so I don't want to do anything.
   ······I understand. Today's meeting was tough, wasn't it?

4. What are you doing at the weekend?
   ······I'm taking the children to Kobe to see the ships.

5. What did you come to study in Japan?
   ······I came to study art.

6. Did you go anywhere for your winter holiday?
   ······Yes, I went skiing in Hokkaido.

Conversation

Separately, please

Yamada: It's twelve o'clock already. Shall we go and have some lunch?

Miller: OK.

Yamada: Where shall we go?

Miller: Hmm...... I'd like to eat something Japanese today.

Yamada: OK, let's go to Tsuruya then.
....

Waitress: What would you like to order?

Miller: The tempura special for me.

Yamada: And I'll have the beef on rice.

Waitress: One tempura special and one beef on rice? Coming right up.
....

Cashier: That's 1,680 yen.

Miller: Sorry, but could we pay separately, please?

Cashier: Of course, the tempura special is 980 yen and the beef on rice is 700 yen.

13

III. Useful Words and Information

MACHI NO NAKA   Town

hakubutsukan	museum	shiyakusho	town hall, city hall
bijutsukan	art museum, art gallery	keisatsusho	police
toshokan	library	kōban	police box
eigakan	cinema, movie theater	shōbōsho	fire station
dōbutsuen	zoo	chūshajō	car park, parking lot
shokubutsuen	botanical garden		
yūenchi	amusement park	daigaku	university
		kōkō	senior high school
o-tera	Buddhist temple	chūgakkō	junior high school
jinja	Shinto shrine	shōgakkō	elementary school
kyōkai	Christian church	yōchien	kindergarten
mosuku	Mosque		
		niku-ya	butcher's shop
taiikukan	gymnasium	pan-ya	bakery
pūru	swimming pool	sakana-ya	fishmonger's, fish store
kōen	park	sakaya	off-licence, liquor store
		yaoya	greengrocer's, fruit and vegetable store
taishikan	embassy		
nyūkoku-kanrikyoku			
	immigration bureau	kissaten	café, coffee shop
		konbini	convenience store
		sūpā	supermarket
		depāto	department store

85

13

IV. Grammar Notes

1. N ga hoshii desu

Hoshii is an i-adjective, and its object is marked by ga.

① Watashi wa tomodachi ga hoshii desu.   I want some friends.

② Ima nani ga ichiban hoshii desu ka.   What do you want most right now?
    ······Kuruma ga hoshii desu.   ······I want a car.

③ Kodomo ga hoshii desu ka.   Do you want to have children?
    ······Iie, hoshikunai desu.   ······No, I don't.

2. V masu-form tai desu

1) V masu-form

The form a verb takes when used with masu (e.g. the kai of kaimasu) is called its masu-form.

2) V masu-form tai desu

The pattern V masu-form tai desu is used to express the speaker's desire to do something. The object of -tai can be marked either with the particle o or with the particle ga. -tai inflects in the same way as i-adjectives.

④ Watashi wa Okinawa e ikitai desu.   I want to go to Okinawa.

⑤ Watashi wa tenpura o tabetai desu.   I'd like to eat some tempura.
    (ga)

⑥ Kōbe de nani o kaitai desu ka.   What do you want to buy in Kobe?
    (ga)
    ······Kutsu o kaitai desu.   ······I want to buy some shoes.
    (ga)

⑦ Onaka ga itai desu kara, nani mo tabetakunai desu.

My stomach hurts, so I don't want to eat anything. (See Lesson 17.)

[Note 1] Hoshii desu and tai desu can only be used when talking about what the speaker or listener wants. They cannot be used to talk about what a third person wants.

[Note 2] Neither hoshii desu ka nor V masu-form tai desu ka should be used when offering someone something or inviting them to do something. For example, kōhii ga hoshii desu ka or kōhii ga nomitai desu ka are not proper ways of asking someone if they would like a cup of coffee. In this case, an expression such as kōhii wa ikaga desu ka or kōhii o nomimasen ka should be used.

3.

> N (place) e { V masu-form / N } ni ikimasu/kimasu/kaerimasu

The purposes of the actions ikimasu, kimasu and kaerimasu are marked by ni.

⑧ Kōbe e Indo-ryōri o tabe ni ikimasu.

I'm going to Kobe to have some Indian food.

When the verb before ni is N-shimasu (e.g. kaimono-shimasu or benkyō-shimasu) or N o shimasu (e.g. o-hanami o shimasu or tsuri o shimasu), it is used in the form N ni ikimasu/kimasu/kaerimasu.

⑨ Kōbe e kaimono ni ikimasu.　　　　I'm going shopping in Kobe.

⑩ Nihon e bijutsu no benkyō ni kimashita.　I came to Japan to study art.

[Note] When a noun denoting an event such as a festival or concert comes before ni, the purpose of the action is usually interpreted as being seeing the festival, listening to the concert, etc.

⑪ Ashita Kyōto no o-matsuri ni ikimasu.

I'm going to see a festival in Kyoto tomorrow.

4. | dokoka/nanika |

Dokoka means 'anywhere' or 'somewhere', and nanika means 'anything' or 'something'. The particle e comes after dokoka and the particle o after nanika, but either of these can be omitted.

⑫ Fuyu-yasumi wa dokoka [e] ikimashita ka.

‥‥‥Hai. Hokkaidō e sukii ni ikimashita.

Did you go anywhere for your winter holiday?

‥‥‥Yes, I went skiing in Hokkaido.

[Note] Wa can be added to a word expressing time in order to make it the topic of a sentence.

⑬ Nodo ga kawakimashita kara, nanika [o] nomitai desu.

I'm thirsty; I'd like something to drink.

5. | go- |

Go- shows respect.

⑭ Go-chūmon wa?　　　　　　May I take your order?

Lesson 14

I. Vocabulary

tsukemasu	II	つけます	turn on
keshimasu	I	けします	turn off
akemasu	II	あけます	open
shimemasu	II	しめます	close, shut
isogimasu	I	いそぎます	hurry
machimasu	I	まちます	wait
mochimasu	I	もちます	hold
torimasu	I	とります	take, pass
tetsudaimasu	I	てつだいます	help (with a task)
yobimasu	I	よびます	call
hanashimasu	I	はなします	speak, talk
tsukaimasu	I	つかいます	use
tomemasu	II	とめます	stop, park
misemasu	II	みせます	show
oshiemasu	II	おしえます	tell [an address]
[jūsho o ～]		[じゅうしょを～]	
suwarimasu	I	すわります	sit down
tachimasu	I *	たちます	stand up
hairimasu	I	はいります	enter [a café]
[kissaten ni ～]		[きっさてんに～]	
demasu	II *	でます	go out [of a café]
[kissaten o ～]		[きっさてんを～]	
furimasu	I	ふります	rain
[ame ga ～]		[あめが～]	
kopii-shimasu	III	コピーします	copy
denki		でんき	electricity, light
eakon		エアコン	air conditioner
pasupōto		パスポート	passport
namae		なまえ	name
jūsho		じゅうしょ	address
chizu		ちず	map
shio		しお	salt
satō		さとう	sugar

mondai	もんだい	question, problem, trouble
kotae	こたえ	answer
yomi-kata	よみかた	how to read, way of reading
-kata	〜かた	how to 〜, way of -ing
massugu	まっすぐ	straight
yukkuri	ゆっくり	slowly, leisurely
sugu	すぐ	immediately
mata	また	again
ato de	あとで	later
mō sukoshi	もう すこし	a little more
mō 〜	もう 〜	〜 more, another 〜

〈Renshū C〉

sā	さあ	right (used when encouraging some course of action)
Are?	あれ？	Oh! Eh? (in surprise or wonder)

〈Kaiwa〉

Shingō o migi e magatte kudasai.	しんごうを みぎへ まがって ください。	Turn right at the traffic lights.
Kore de onegai-shimasu.	これで おねがいします。	I'd like to pay with this.
otsuri	おつり	change

....

Midori-chō	みどりちょう	a fictitious town

89

14

II. Translation

Sentence Patterns

1. Just a moment, please.
2. Shall I carry your bag?
3. Mr. Miller's making a phone call now.

Example Sentences

1. Please write your name with a ballpoint pen.
   ······Yes, OK.

2. Excuse me, could you tell me how to read this kanji, please?
   ······It's 'jusho'.

3. Hot, isn't it? Shall I open the window?
   ······Yes, please.

4. Shall I come to the station to meet you?
   ······No, it's fine. I'll get a taxi.

5. Where's Ms. Sato?
   ······She's in the meeting room, talking to Mr. Matsumoto.
   OK, I'll come back later.

6. Is it raining?
   ······No, it isn't [raining].

Conversation

To Midoricho, please

Karina: To Midoricho, please.
Driver: OK.

....

Karina: Excuse me. Please turn right at those lights.
Driver: Right, yes?
Karina: Yes.

....

Driver: Is it straight on?
Karina: Yes, go straight on, please.

....

Karina: Please stop in front of that flower shop.
Driver: OK.
       It's 1,800 yen.
Karina: Take it out of this, please.
Driver: Here's 3,200 yen change. Thank you.

III. Useful Words and Information

EKI　Station

kippu-uriba	ticket office, ticket area
jidō-kenbaiki	ticket machine
seisanki	fare adjustment machine
kaisatsuguchi	ticket barrier
deguchi	exit
iriguchi	entrance
higashi-guchi	east exit
nishi-guchi	west exit
minami-guchi	south exit
kita-guchi	north exit
chūō-guchi	central exit
[puratto]hōmu	platform
baiten	kiosk
koin-rokkā	coin locker
takushii-noriba	taxi rank
basu-tāminaru	bus terminal
basutei	bus stop

tokkyū	super-express train
kyūkō	express train
kaisoku	rapid service train
junkyū	semi-express train
futsū	local train
jikokuhyō	timetable
-hatsu	departing ~
-chaku	arriving at ~
[Tōkyō]-iki	for [TOKYO]
teikiken	season ticket, commuter pass
kaisūken	coupon ticket
katamichi	one way
ōfuku	return/round trip

91

14

IV. Grammar Notes

1. Verb Groups

Japanese verbs conjugate, and sentences with various meanings can be formed by adding various phrases to the conjugated forms of the verbs. Verbs are classified into three groups depending on how they are conjugated.

1) Group I Verbs

In all verbs of this group, the last sound of the masu-form is from the i-column of the syllabary chart, e.g. kakimasu (write), nomimasu (drink).

2) Group II verbs

In most verbs of this group, the last sound of the masu-form is from the e-column (e.g. tabemasu (eat) and misemasu (show)), but in some verbs it is a sound from the i-column (e.g. mimasu (see)).

3) Group III Verbs

Verbs of this group include shimasu and 'action-denoting noun + shimasu', as well as kimasu.

2. V te-form

The verb form that ends with te or de is called the te-form. The method by which the te-form is created from the masu-form depends on the group to which the verb belongs, as described below. (See Exercise A1, Lesson14 of Main Text.)

1) Group I Verbs

   (1) When the last sound of the masu-form is the vowel i, chi or ri, the i, chi or ri is dropped and tte is attached.   e.g. kaimasu → katte buy
   machimasu → matte wait   kaerimasu → kaette go home, return

   (2) When the last sound of the masu-form is mi, bi or ni, the mi, bi or ni is dropped and nde is attached.   e.g. nomimasu → nonde drink
   yobimasu → yonde call   shinimasu → shinde die

   (3) When the last sound of the masu-form is ki or gi, the ki or gi is dropped and ite or ide respectively is attached.
   e.g. kakimasu → kaite write   isogimasu → isoide hurry
   However ikimasu (go) is an exception, and becomes itte.

   (4) When the last sound of the masu-form is shi, te is added to the masu-form.
   e.g. kashimasu → kashite lend

2) Group II Verbs

Te is added to the masu-form.   e.g. tabemasu → tabete eat
misemasu → misete show   mimasu → mite see

3) Group III Verbs

Te is added to the masu-form.   e.g. kimasu → kite come
shimasu → shite do   sanpo-shimasu → sanpo-shite go for a walk

3. | V te-form kudasai | Please do......

This sentence pattern is used to tell, request or invite the listener to do something.

14

However, it is not a very polite way of asking someone to do something, so it is often used together with the expression sumimasen ga as in ① below.

①　Sumimasen ga, kono kanji no yomi-kata o oshiete kudasai.
　　Excuse me, could you tell me how to read this kanji, please? (Requesting)

②　Bōrupen de namae o kaite kudasai.
　　Please write your name with a ballpoint pen. (Telling)

③　Dōzo takusan tabete kudasai.　Please eat as much as you want. (Inviting)

4.　| **V te-form　imasu** |

This sentence pattern indicates that a certain action or motion is in progress.

④　Mirā-san wa ima denwa o kakete imasu.
　　Mr. Miller is making a phone call now.

⑤　Ima ame ga futte imasu ka.　　　　　　Is it raining now?
　　……Hai, futte imasu.　　　　　　　　……Yes, it is [raining].
　　……Iie, futte imasen.　　　　　　　　……No, it isn't [raining].

5.　| **V masu-form mashō ka** |　　Shall I……?

This expression is used when the speaker is offering to do something for the listener.

⑥　Ashita mo kimashō ka.　　　　　　　Shall I come tomorrow, too?
　　……Ē, 10-ji ni kite kudasai.　　　　　……Yes, please come at ten.

⑦　Kasa o kashimashō ka.　　　　　　　Shall I lend you my umbrella?
　　……Sumimasen. Onegai-shimasu.　　　……Yes, please.

⑧　Nimotsu o mochimashō ka.　　　　　Shall I carry your bag?
　　……Iie, kekkō desu.　　　　　　　　……No, thank you.

6.　| **N ga　V** |

When describing a phenomenon by saying what was felt about it through one or more of the five senses (sight, hearing, etc.) or when telling someone objectively about an event, the subject is marked with the particle ga.

⑨　Ame ga futte imasu.　　　　　　　　It's raining.

⑩　Mirā-san ga imasen ne.　　　　　　Mr. Miller isn't here, is he?

7.　| **sumimasen ga** |

⑪　Sumimasen ga, shio o totte kudasai.
　　Excuse me, could you pass the salt, please?

⑫　Shitsurei desu ga, o-namae wa?　　　Excuse me, but what is your name?

The ga in expressions such as sumimasen ga and shitsurei desu ga (used as introductory remarks when addressing someone) is not being used in an antithetical sense but as a casual preamble to a remark.

Lesson 15

I. Vocabulary

okimasu I	おきます	put
tsukurimasu I	つくります	make, produce
urimasu I	うります	sell
shirimasu I	しります	get to know
sumimasu I	すみます	be going to live
kenkyū-shimasu III	けんきゅうします	do research
shiryō	しりょう	materials, data
katarogu	カタログ	catalogue
jikokuhyō	じこくひょう	timetable
fuku	ふく	clothes
seihin	せいひん	products
sofuto	ソフト	software
denshi-jisho	でんしじしょ	electronic dictionary
keizai	けいざい	economy
shiyakusho	しやくしょ	municipal office, city hall
kōkō	こうこう	senior high school
haisha	はいしゃ	dentist, dentist's
dokushin	どくしん	single, unmarried
sumimasen	すみません	I'm sorry.

⟨Renshū C⟩

minasan	みなさん	Ladies and Gentlemen, everybody

⟨Kaiwa⟩

omoidashimasu　Ⅰ	おもいだします	remember, recollect
irasshaimasu　Ⅰ	いらっしゃいます	be (honorific equivalent of imasu)

....

Nipponbashi	にっぽんばし	a shopping district in Osaka
Minna no intabyū	みんなの インタビュー	a fictitious TV programme

15

II. Translation

Sentence Patterns
1. Is it all right to take photographs?
2. Mr. Santos has an electronic dictionary.

Example Sentences
1. May I have this catalogue, please?
   ······Yes, of course. Please help yourself.

2. May I borrow this dictionary?
   ······Sorry, I'm using it at the moment.

3. You mustn't play here.
   ······Okay.

4. Do you know the ward office's telephone number?
   ······No, I don't.

5. Where does Maria live?
   ······She lives in Osaka.

6. Is Mr. Wang married?
   ······No, he's single.

7. What job do you do?
   ······I'm a teacher. I teach in a secondary school.

Conversation
What family do you have?

Kimura: Good film, wasn't it?

Miller: Yes. It made me think of my family.

Kimura: Oh? What family do you have?

Miller: My parents and one elder sister.

Kimura: Where are they?

15

Miller: My parents live near New York.
My sister works in London.
How about your family, Ms. Kimura?

Kimura: There are three of us. My father is a bank official.
My mother teaches English in a secondary school.

III. Useful Words and Information

SHOKUGYŌ   Occupations

kaishain company employee	**kōmuin** civil servant, public servant	**ekiin** station attendant	**ginkōin** bank employee	**yūbinkyokuin** postman
ten'in shop assistant	**chōrishi** cook	**riyōshi** barber **biyōshi** beautician	**kyōshi** teacher	**bengoshi** solicitor, lawyer
kenkyūsha research worker	**isha/kangoshi** doctor/nurse	**untenshu** driver	**keisatsukan** policeman	**gaikōkan** diplomat
seijika politician	**gaka** painter	**sakka** author	**ongakuka** musician	**kenchikuka** architect
enjinia engineer	**dezainā** designer	**jānarisuto** journalist	**kashu/haiyū** singer/actor	**supōtsu-senshu** athlete

15

IV. Grammar Notes

1. | **V te-form mo ii desu ka** | May I do......?

This sentence pattern is used for asking permission to do something.

① Shashin o totte mo ii desu ka.   May I take a photo?

② and ③ illustrate how to respond when your permission is sought using this pattern. When withholding permission or stating that something is prohibited, an apologetic or euphemistic answer may be given, or the reason may be given, as illustrated in ② (with holding permission,) and ③ and 2 (stating that something is prohibited) below.

② Koko de tabako o sutte mo ii desu ka.   May I smoke here?
   ······Ē, [sutte mo] ii desu yo.   ······Yes, you may [smoke].
   ······Sumimasen, chotto······. Nodo ga itai desu kara.
   ······Sorry, I'd prefer it if you didn't. I've got a sore throat. (See Lessson 17.)

③ Koko de tabako o sutte mo ii desu ka.   Is it all right to smoke here?
   ······Ē, [sutte mo] ii desu yo.   ······Yes, it's fine [to smoke].
   ······Iie, [sutte wa] ikemasen. Kin'en desu kara.
   ······No, it isn't. It's a No Smoking area.

2. | **V te-form wa ikemasen** | You must not do......

This sentence pattern is used to express prohibition.

④ Koko de tabako o sutte wa ikemasen. Kin'en desu kara.
   You can't smoke here; it's a No Smoking area.

This expression cannot be used by someone of lower status to someone of higher status.

3. | **V te-form imasu** |

This sentence pattern is used in the ways illustrated below, in addition to expressing a continuing action as explained in Lesson 14.

1) To show a state (mainly with verbs used in the -te imasu form)

⑤ Watashi wa kekkon-shite imasu.   I'm married.

⑥ Watashi wa Tanaka-san o shitte imasu.   I know Mr. Tanaka.

⑦ Watashi wa kamera o motte imasu.   I have a camera.

⑧ Watashi wa Ōsaka ni sunde imasu.   I live in Osaka.

[Note 1] The negative of shitte imasu is shirimasen. Be careful not to say shitte imasen.

⑨ Shiyakusho no denwa-bangō o shitte imasu ka.
   Do you know the number of City Hall?

   ······Hai, shitte imasu.   ······Yes, I do.
   ······Iie, shirimasen.   ······No, I don't.

[Note 2] The phrase motte imasu can mean either having something with you at the moment, or owning it.

2) To show a habitual action (the same action repeated over a long period), occupation or personal status.

⑩ IMC wa konpyūtā-sofuto o tsukutte imasu.
IMC produces computer software.

⑪ Sūpā de nanpurā o utte imasu.　　　　Supermarkets sell nam pla.

⑫ Mirā-san wa IMC de hataraite imasu.　　Mr. Miller works at IMC.

⑬ Imōto wa daigaku de benkyō-shite imasu.
My younger sister is studying at university.

4. | N ni V |

The particle ni is used with verbs such as hairimasu, suwarimasu, norimasu (ride; see Lesson 16), noborimasu (climb, go up; see Lesson 19) and tsukimasu (arrive; see Lesson 25) to indicate the location of the subject resulting from the action expressed by the verb.

⑭ Koko ni haitte wa ikemasen.　　　　You can't come in here.

⑮ Koko ni suwatte mo ii desu ka.　　　May I sit here?

⑯ Kyōto-eki kara 16-ban no basu ni notte kudasai.
Take the Number 16 bus from Kyoto Station. (See Lesson 16.)

99

5. | N₁ ni N₂ o V |

The particle ni indicates the location (N₁) of N₂ as the result of an action.

⑰ Koko ni kuruma o tomete kudasai.　　Stop the car here, please.
The ni in ⑱ has the same function.

⑱ Koko ni jūsho o kaite kudasai.　　　Write your address here, please.

15

Lesson 16

I. Vocabulary

norimasu I	のります	ride, get on [a train]
[densha ni 〜]	［でんしゃに〜］	
orimasu II	おります	get off [a train]
[densha o 〜]	［でんしゃを〜］	
norikaemasu II	のりかえます	change (train, etc.)
abimasu II	あびます	take [a shower]
[shawā o 〜]	［シャワーを〜］	
iremasu II	いれます	put in, insert
dashimasu I	だします	take out, hand in, send
oroshimasu I	おろします	withdraw
[okane o 〜]	［おかねを〜］	
hairimasu I	はいります	enter [university]
[daigaku ni 〜]	［だいがくに〜］	
demasu II	でます	graduate from [university]
[daigaku o 〜]	［だいがくを〜］	
oshimasu I	おします	push, press
nomimasu I	のみます	drink alcohol
hajimemasu II	はじめます	start, begin
kengaku-shimasu III	けんがくします	tour, visit a place to study it
denwa-shimasu III	でんわします	phone
wakai	わかい	young
nagai	ながい	long
mijikai	みじかい	short
akarui	あかるい	bright, light
kurai	くらい	dark
karada*	からだ	body, health
atama	あたま	head, brain
kami	かみ	hair
kao*	かお	face
me	め	eye
mimi*	みみ	ear
hana*	はな	nose
kuchi*	くち	mouth
ha*	は	tooth
onaka*	おなか	stomach
ashi*	あし	leg, foot
se	せ	height

sābisu	サービス	service
jogingu	ジョギング	jogging（〜 o shimasu：jog）
shawā	シャワー	shower
midori	みどり	green, greenery
[o-]tera	［お］てら	Buddhist temple
jinja	じんじゃ	Shinto shrine
-ban	−ばん	number −
dōyatte	どうやって	in what way, how
dono 〜	どの 〜	which 〜（used for three or more）
dore	どれ	which one（of three or more things）

〈Renshū C〉

Sugoi desu ne.	すごいですね。	That's amazing!
[Iie,] madamada desu.	［いいえ，］まだまだです。	[No,] I still have a long way to go.

〈Kaiwa〉

O-hikidashi desu ka.	おひきだしですか。	Are you making a withdrawal?
mazu	まず	first of all
tsugi ni	つぎに	next, as a next step
kyasshu-kādo	キャッシュカード	cash dispensing card
anshō-bangō	あんしょうばんごう	personal identification number, PIN
kingaku	きんがく	amount of money
kakunin	かくにん	confirmation（-shimasu：confirm）
botan	ボタン	button

....

JR	JR	Japan Railways
Yuki-matsuri	ゆきまつり	Snow Festival
Bandon	バンドン	Bandung（in Indonesia）
Furanken	フランケン	Franken（in Germany）
Berakurusu	ベラクルス	Veracruz（in Mexico）
Umeda	うめだ	a district in Osaka
Daigaku-mae	だいがくまえ	a fictitious bus stop

16

II. Translation

Sentence Patterns
1. In the mornings, I go jogging, have a shower, and then go to work.
2. After the concert was over, we had a meal in a restaurant.
3. The food in Osaka is very good.
4. This room is big and bright.

Example Sentences
1. What did you do yesterday?
   ······I went to the library, borrowed a book, and then met some friends.

2. How do you get to the University?
   ······I get on the number 16 bus at Kyoto station and get off at Daigakumae.

3. Are you going to look round Osaka Castle now?
   ······No, we're going there after lunch.

4. Which is Maria?
   ······She's the one with long hair over there.

5. Which is Taro's bike?
   ······It's that new blue one.

6. What sort of city is Nara?
   ······It's a quiet, beautiful city.

7. Who's that person over there?
   ······That's Karina. She's Indonesian, and she's a student at Fuji University.

Conversation
Please show me how to use it

Maria:	Excuse me, could you show me how to use this, please?
Bank official:	Do you want to take some money out?
Maria:	Yes.
Bank official:	Right, start by pressing here, please.
Maria:	OK.
Bank official:	Then put your cash card in here and type in your pin number.
Maria:	OK.
	I've done that.
Bank official:	OK, now press the amount you want.
Maria:	I want 50,000 yen, so 5······
Bank official:	Press this 'Man (10,000)' key and the 'En (YEN)' key here.
	Then press this 'Kakunin (CONFIRM)' button.
Maria:	Yes. Thank you very much.

16

III. Useful Words and Information

ATM NO TSUKAI-KATA How to Use a Cash Machine

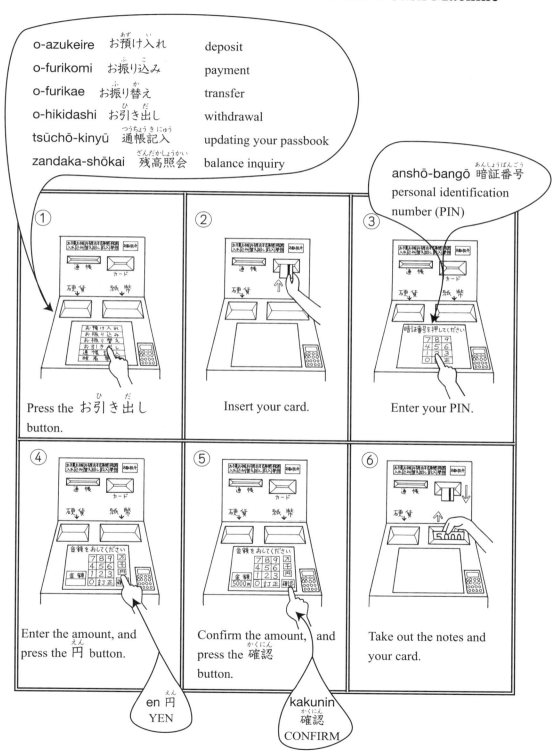

o-azukeire お預け入れ — deposit
o-furikomi お振り込み — payment
o-furikae お振り替え — transfer
o-hikidashi お引き出し — withdrawal
tsūchō-kinyū 通帳記入 — updating your passbook
zandaka-shōkai 残高照会 — balance inquiry

anshō-bangō 暗証番号
personal identification number (PIN)

① Press the お引き出し button.

② Insert your card.

③ Enter your PIN.

④ Enter the amount, and press the 円 button.

⑤ Confirm the amount, and press the 確認 button.

⑥ Take out the notes and your card.

en 円 YEN

kakunin 確認 CONFIRM

16

IV. Grammar Notes

1. How to join two or more sentences together

Two or more sentences can be joined together using -te (de).

1) V₁ te-form, [V₂ te-form,] V₃

When mentioning two or more actions that take place in succession, they are listed in their order of occurrence using the te-form. The tense of the sentence is determined by the tense form of the last verb in the sentence.

① Asa jogingu o shite, shawā o abite, kaisha e ikimasu.
In the mornings, I go jogging, take a shower, and then go to work.

② Kōbe e itte, eiga o mite, ocha o nomimashita.
I went to Kobe, where I saw a movie and drank some tea.

2) i-adj (～ǐ) → ～ kute

ōki - i →	ōki - kute	big
chiisa - i →	chiisa - kute	small
i - i →	yo - kute (exception)	good

③ Mirā-san wa wakakute, genki desu.   Mr. Miller is young and energetic.

④ Kinō wa tenki ga yokute, atsukatta desu.   It was fine and hot yesterday.

3) na-adj [ná] → ～ de

⑤ Mirā-san wa hansamu de, shinsetsu desu.   Mr. Miller is handsome and kind.

⑥ Nara wa shizuka de, kireina machi desu.   Nara is a quiet, beautiful city.

[Note] -te (de) cannot be used to connect two adjective sentences having the same subject if they present two contrasting descriptions. In such a case, ga is used (see Lesson 8-4).

× Kono heya wa semakute, kirei desu.

○ Kono heya wa semai desu ga, kirei desu.   This room is small but clean.

4) N de

⑦ Karina-san wa Indoneshia-jin de, Fuji-daigaku no ryūgakusei desu.
Karina is Indonesian; she's a student at Fuji University.

⑧ Karina-san wa gakusei de, Maria-san wa shufu desu.
Karina is a student, and Maria is a housewife.

2. │ V₁ te-form kara, V₂ │

In this sentence pattern, V₂ expresses something done after V₁. Because of this, V₁ is often a precondition of doing V₂ or an action preparatory to doing it. The tense of the sentence is determined by the tense of the last verb in the sentence.

⑨ Okane o irete kara, botan o oshite kudasai.
Put the money in, please, and then press the button.

The subject of V te-form kara is marked with the particle ga.

⑩　Mō hirugohan o tabemashita ka.　　Have you already had your lunch?
　　　······Kono shigoto ga owatte kara, tabemasu.
　　　······No, I'm going to have it when I've finished this job.

3. N₁ wa N₂ ga adj

This sentence pattern indicates that the topic (N₁) has the characteristic 'N₂ ga adj'.

⑪　Ōsaka wa tabemono ga oishii desu.　　The food in Osaka is very good.

⑫　Doitsu no Furanken wa wain ga yūmei desu.
　　Franken in Germany is famous for its wine.

⑬　Maria-san wa kami ga nagai desu.　　Maria has long hair.

4. N o V

Verbs such as demasu and orimasu, are used together with the particle o, which indicates a starting point.

⑭　7-ji ni uchi o demasu.　　　　　　I leave home at seven.

⑮　Umeda de densha o orimashita.　　I got off the train at Umeda.

5. dōyatte

Dōyatte is used when asking the way or how to do something.

⑯　Daigaku made dōyatte ikimasu ka.
　　How do you get to the University?
　　　······Kyōto-eki kara 16-ban no basu ni notte, Daigaku-mae de orimasu.
　　　······I take the Number 16 bus from Kyoto Station and get off at Daigakumae.

6. dore/dono N

Dore is an interrogative used when asking someone to specify one item out of a list of three or more .

⑰　Mirā-san no kasa wa dore desu ka.　　Which is Mr. Miller's umbrella?
　　　······Ano aoi kasa desu.　　　　　　······It's that blue one.

Dore cannot modify a noun directly. When modifying a noun, dono is used.

⑱　Santosu-san wa dono hito desu ka.　　Which is Mr. Santos?
　　　······Ano se ga takakute, kami ga kuroi hito desu.
　　　······That tall, black-haired man.

Lesson 17

I. Vocabulary

oboemasu	II	おぼえます	memorise
wasuremasu	II	わすれます	forget
nakushimasu	I	なくします	lose
haraimasu	I	はらいます	pay
kaeshimasu	I	かえします	give back, return
dekakemasu	II	でかけます	go out
nugimasu	I	ぬぎます	take off (clothes, shoes, etc.)
motte ikimasu	I	もって いきます	take (something)
motte kimasu	III	もって きます	bring (something)
shinpai-shimasu	III	しんぱいします	worry
zangyō-shimasu	III	ざんぎょうします	work overtime
shutchō-shimasu	III	しゅっちょうします	go on a business trip
nomimasu	I	のみます	take [medicine]
[kusuri o ～]		[くすりを～]	
hairimasu	I	はいります	take [a bath]
[o-furo ni ～]		[おふろに～]	
taisetsu[na]		たいせつ[な]	important, precious
daijōbu[na]		だいじょうぶ[な]	all right
abunai		あぶない	dangerous
kin'en		きんえん	no smoking
[kenkō-]		[けんこう]	[health] insurance card
hokenshō		ほけんしょう	
netsu		ねつ	temperature, fever
byōki		びょうき	illness, disease
kusuri		くすり	medicine
[o-]furo		[お]ふろ	bath
uwagi		うわぎ	jacket, outerwear
shitagi		したぎ	underwear

2, 3-nichi	2、3 にち	two or three days
2, 3-	2、3〜	two or three 〜 (where 〜 is a counter suffix)
〜 made ni	〜までに	before 〜, by 〜 (indicating time limit)
desukara	ですから	therefore, so

〈Kaiwa〉

Dō shimashita ka.	どう しましたか。	What's the matter?
nodo	のど	throat
[〜 ga] itai desu.	[〜が] いたいです。	(I) have a pain [in my 〜].
kaze	かぜ	cold, flu
sorekara	それから	and, furthermore
Odaiji ni.	おだいじに。	Take care of yourself. (said to people who are ill)

17

II. Translation

Sentence Patterns

1. Please don't take photographs.
2. You have to show your passport.
3. I don't have to get up early on Sundays.

Example Sentences

1. Please don't park there.
   ······Sorry.

2. It's already midnight. Will you be all right on your own?
   ······Yes, please don't worry; I'll take a taxi home.

3. Shall we go out for a drink tonight?
   ······Sorry, I have to go on a business trip to Hong Kong tomorrow, so I'm going home early.

4. Do children have to pay, too?
   ······No, they don't [have to pay].

5. When does the report have to be handed in by?
   ······[Hand it in] by Friday, please.

Conversation

What seems to be the matter?

Doctor:	What seems to be the matter?
Matsumoto:	I've had a sore throat since yesterday, and I've also got a slight temperature.
Doctor:	I see. Say, "Aah", please. (lit:Open your mouth a moment, please.)

···

Doctor:	You've caught a cold, haven't you? Please take it easy for two or three days.
Matsumoto:	Yes, but I have to go to Tokyo on business tomorrow.
Doctor:	OK, please take your medicine and go to bed early today.
Matsumoto:	All right.
Doctor:	And please don't have a bath tonight, OK?
Matsumoto:	Yes, I understand.
Doctor:	Right you are then, look after yourself.
Matsumoto:	Thank you very much.

17

III. Useful Words and Information

KARADA · BYŌKI   Body and Illness

Dō shimashita ka.	What seems to be the problem?
atama ga itai	have a headache
onaka ga itai	have a stomachache
ha ga itai	have a toothache
netsu ga arimasu	have a temperature, fever
seki ga demasu	have a cough
hanamizu ga demasu	have a runny nose
chi ga demasu	bleed
hakike ga shimasu	feel sick, nauseous
samuke ga shimasu	feel a chill
memai ga shimasu	feel dizzy
geri o shimasu	have diarrhoea
benpi o shimasu	be constipated
kega o shimasu	get injured
yakedo o shimasu	get burnt
shokuyoku ga arimasen	have no appetite
kata ga korimasu	feel stiff in one's shoulders
karada ga darui	feel weary
kayui	itchy

kao atama me hana kami kuchi mimi nodo ago mune kata kubi yubi ude te hiji senaka tsume hiza onaka koshi hone ashi shiri

17

kaze	cold
infuruenza	flu, influenza
mōchō	appendicitis

gikkurigoshi	slipped disc
nenza	sprain
kossetsu	bone fracture
futsukayoi	hangover

IV. Grammar Notes

1. V nai-form

The form of a verb that attaches to nai (e.g. kaka in kakanai) is called its nai-form. The method by which the nai-form is created from the masu-form depends on the group to which the verb belongs, as explained below. (See Exercise A1, Lesson 17 of Main Text.)

1) Group I Verbs

The final sound of the masu-form of verbs in this group is always from the i-column, and this is changed to the corresponding syllable from the a-column to make the nai-form. However, with verbs where the final sound is the vowel i (e.g. kaimasu and aimasu), this changes not to a but to wa.

kaki-masu	→	kaka-nai	isogi-masu	→	isoga-nai
yomi-masu	→	yoma-nai	asobi-masu	→	asoba-nai
tori-masu	→	tora-nai	machi-masu	→	mata-nai
sui-masu	→	suwa-nai	hanashi-masu	→	hanasa-nai

2) Group II Verbs

The nai-form of verbs in this group is the same as their masu-form.

| tabe-masu | → | tabe-nai |
| mi-masu | → | mi-nai |

3) Group III Verbs

benkyō-shi-masu	→	benkyō-shi-nai
shi-masu	→	shi-nai
ki-masu	→	ko-nai

2. | V nai-form nai de kudasai | Please don't do......

This sentence pattern is used to ask or tell someone not to do something.

① Koko de shashin o toranai de kudasai.

Please don't take photographs here.

It can also be used to show consideration to someone by telling them they don't have to do something.

② Watashi wa genki desu kara, shinpai-shinai de kudasai.

I'm fine, so please don't worry about me.

3. | V nai-form nakereba narimasen | Must do......

This sentence pattern is used to say that something must be done. Note that it is not in the negative.

③ Kusuri o nomanakereba narimasen.   I must take some medicine.

4. V nai-form nakute mo ii desu Need not do......

This sentence pattern is used when saying that it is not necessary to do something.

④ Ashita konakute mo ii desu. You don't have to come tomorrow.

5. Making an object the topic of a sentence

When making a noun in the expression N o V (i.e. a noun that is the direct object of a verb) into the topic of a sentence, the noun is placed at the beginning of the sentence and the particle o is replaced by the particle wa.

Koko ni   nimotsu o okanai de kudasai.   Don't put your bags here, please.

Nimotsu o̶ wa koko ni   okanai de kudasai.

⑤ Nimotsu <u>wa</u>   koko ni   okanai de kudasai.   Don't put your bags here, please.

Kaisha no   shokudō de hirugohan o tabemasu.
I have lunch in the company cafeteria.

Hirugohan o̶ wa kaisha no   shokudō de tabemasu.

⑥ Hirugohan <u>wa</u>   kaisha no   shokudō de tabemasu.
I have lunch in the company cafeteria.

6. N (time) made ni V

This indicates a time by which an event will end or an action must be completed.

⑦ Kaigi wa 5-ji made ni owarimasu. The meeting will end by five.

⑧ Do-yōbi made ni hon o kaesanakereba narimasen.
I have to return the book by Saturday.

[Note] The particle made explained in Lesson 4 indicates the end point of a continuing action. Be careful not to confuse it with made ni.

⑨ 5-ji made hatarakimasu. I work until five o'clock.

111

17

Lesson 18

I. Vocabulary

dekimasu	II	できます	be able to, can
araimasu	I	あらいます	wash
hikimasu	I	ひきます	play (stringed instrument, piano, etc.)
utaimasu	I	うたいます	sing
atsumemasu	II	あつめます	collect, gather
sutemasu	II	すてます	throw away
kaemasu	II	かえます	exchange, change
unten-shimasu	III	うんてんします	drive
yoyaku-shimasu	III	よやくします	reserve, book
piano		ピアノ	piano
-mētoru		ーメートル	－ meter
genkin		げんきん	cash
shumi		しゅみ	hobby
nikki		にっき	diary
oinori		おいのり	prayer（〜 o shimasu：pray）
kachō		かちょう	section head
buchō		ぶちょう	department head
shachō*		しゃちょう	company president
dōbutsu		どうぶつ	animal
uma		うま	horse
intānetto		インターネット	the Internet

112

18

〈Kaiwa〉

tokuni	とくに	especially
hē	へえ	What! Really! (used when expressing surprise)
Sore wa omoshiroi desu ne.	それは おもしろい ですね。	That's interesting, isn't it?
nakanaka	なかなか	not easily (used with negatives)
Hontō desu ka.	ほんとうですか。	Really?
zehi	ぜひ	by all means, really

....

Furusato	ふるさと	Furusato (a song title meaning 'Home Town')
Biitoruzu	ビートルズ	the Beatles (a famous British pop group)
Akihabara	あきはばら	a district in Tokyo

18

II. Translation

Sentence Patterns

1. Mr. Miller can read kanji.
2. I like watching films. [lit: My hobby is watching films.]
3. I always write something in my diary before I go to sleep.

Example Sentences

1. Can you drive?
   ······Yes, I can.

2. Can you ride a bike, Maria?
   ······No, I can't.

3. What time is Osaka Castle open until?
   ······[Until] five o'clock.

4. Can I pay by card?
   ······I'm sorry, we only take cash.

5. What are you interested in? [lit: What are your hobbies?]
   ······I collect old clocks.

6. Do Japanese children have to learn hiragana before they start school?
   ······No, they don't [have to learn it].

7. Please take this medicine before meals.
   ······Yes, I understand.

8. When did you get married?
   ······[I got married] three years ago.

Conversation

What do you like doing? [lit: What are your hobbies?]

Yamada: What do you like doing, Mr. Santos?

Santos: Photography.

Yamada: What kind of photographs do you take?

Santos: Photographs of animals. I particularly like horses.

Yamada: Really? How interesting!
Have you photographed any horses since coming to Japan?

Santos: No.
You don't see many horses in Japan.

Yamada: There are a lot of horses in Hokkaido, you know.

Santos: Really?
In that case, I definitely want to go there during my summer holiday.

III. Useful Words and Information

UGOKI   Actions

tobu fly	tobu jump	noboru climb	hashiru run
oyogu swim	moguru dive	tobikomu dive into	sakadachi-suru do a handstand
hau crawl	keru kick	furu wave	mochiageru lift
nageru throw	tataku pat, tap	hiku pull	osu push
mageru bend	nobasu extend	korobu fall down	furimuku look back

115

18

IV. Grammar Notes

1. Dictionary form of verbs

This is the basic form of a verb, as given in the dictionary. The method by which the dictionary form is created from the masu-form depends on which group the verb belongs to, as explained below. (See Exercise A1, Lesson 18, Main Textbook.)

1) Group I verbs

With verbs in this group, the last sound of the masu-form, which is always in the i-column, is changed to a corresponding sound in the u-column.

kaki-masu	→	kaku	isogi-masu	→	isogu
yomi-masu	→	yomu	asobi-masu	→	asobu
tori-masu	→	toru	machi-masu	→	matsu
sui-masu	→	suu	hanashi-masu	→	hanasu

2) Group II verbs

Ru is added to the masu-form.

tabe-masu	→	tabe-ru
mi-masu	→	mi-ru

3) Group III verbs

The dictionary form of shimasu is suru, while that of kimasu is kuru.

2.

N V-dictionary form koto } ga dekimasu	Can do......

Dekimasu is a verb that indicates that a person has the ability to do something or that some behaviour is possible as a result of the situation. The object of dekimasu is marked by ga, and the ability or what is possible is expressed in the form of either a noun or the dictionary form of a verb with koto added to it.

1) In the case of a noun

Nouns indicating motion, such as (unten, kaimono, sukii and dansu) can be used, as can nouns representing an ability, such as Nihon-go or piano.

① Mirā-san wa Nihon-go ga dekimasu.

Mr. Miller can speak Japanese.

② Yuki ga takusan furimashita kara, kotoshi wa sukii ga dekimasu.

A lot of snow has fallen, so we can ski this year.

2) In the case of a verb

When a verb is used to describe an ability or possibility, koto is attached to the verb's dictionary form to make it a noun phrase, which is then followed by ga dekimasu.

③ Mirā-san wa <u>kanji o yomu koto</u> ga dekimasu.   Mr. Miller can read kanji.
               (noun phrase)

④ <u>Kādo de harau koto</u> ga dekimasu.   You can pay by card.
     (noun phrase)

18

3.

| Watashi no shumi wa | N
V-dictionary form koto | desu | My interest is...... |

⑤ Watashi no shumi wa ongaku desu.　　　I'm interested in music.

Using the V-dictionary form koto enables the interest to be described more specifically than just using a noun.

⑥ Watashi no shumi wa ongaku o kiku koto desu.　 I like listening to music.

4.

| V₁-dictionary form
N no
Quantifier (time period) | mae ni, V₂ | ......before...... |

1) Verb

This sentence pattern shows that V_2 occurs before V_1. Note that V_1 always takes the dictionary form whether the tense of the sentence (i.e. the tense of V_2) is past or non-past.

⑦ Nihon e kuru mae ni, Nihon-go o benkyō-shimashita.

I studied Japanese before coming to Japan.

⑧ Neru mae ni, hon o yomimasu.　　　I read a book before going to bed.

2) Noun

No is added after the noun. Nouns expressing motion can be used.

⑨ Shokuji no mae ni, te o araimasu.　　　I wash my hands before eating.

3) Quantifier (time period)

Note that no is not added to a quantifier (time period).

⑩ Tanaka-san wa 1-jikan mae ni, dekakemashita.　 Mr. Tanaka went out one hour ago.

5.　nakanaka

When nakanaka is followed by a negative expression, it means 'not easily' or 'not as expected'.

⑪ Nihon de wa nakanaka uma o miru koto ga dekimasen.

You don't see many horses in Japan.

[Note] Example sentence　⑪　(see Conversation, Lesson 18 of Main Text) takes Nihon de as its topic. When a noun with de attached is taken as the topic in this way, it becomes N de wa . (See Article 1 for what happens when words with particles other than ga and o are taken as sentence topics.)

6.　zehi

Zehi is used by speakers to intensify their expressions of hope.

⑫ Zehi Hokkaidō e ikitai desu.　　　I really want to go to Hokkaido.

⑬ Zehi asobi ni kite kudasai.　　　Do please come and visit me.

Lesson 19

I. Vocabulary

noborimasu	I	のぼります	climb, go up
tomarimasu	I	とまります	stay [at a hotel]
[hoteru ni 〜]		［ホテルに〜］	
sōji-shimasu	III	そうじします	clean (a room)
sentaku-shimasu	III	せんたくします	wash (clothes)
narimasu	I	なります	become
nemui		ねむい	sleepy
tsuyoi		つよい	strong
yowai*		よわい	weak
renshū		れんしゅう	practice (〜 [o] -shimasu : practise)
gorufu		ゴルフ	golf (〜 o shimasu : play golf)
sumō		すもう	sumo wrestling (〜 o shimasu : wrestle)
ocha		おちゃ	tea ceremony
hi		ひ	day, date
chōshi		ちょうし	condition
ichido		いちど	once
ichido mo		いちども	not once, never (used with negatives)
dandan		だんだん	gradually
mōsugu		もうすぐ	soon
okagesama de		おかげさまで	Thank you. (used when expressing gratitude for help received)
demo		でも	but

118

〈Kaiwa〉

kanpai	かんぱい	Bottoms up./Cheers!
daietto	ダイエット	diet（〜 o shimasu：go on a diet）
muri[na]	むり[な]	excessive, impossible
karada ni ii	からだに いい	good for one's health

....

Tōkyō Sukaitsurii	とうきょうスカイツリー	Tokyo Sky Tree（broadcasting tower with observation deck in Tokyo）
Katsushika Hokusai	かつしかほくさい	a famous Edo-period woodblock artist and painter（1760-1849）

19

II. Translation

Sentence Patterns

1. I've been to see sumo.
2. On my days off, I do things like playing tennis and going for a walk.
3. It's going to get hotter and hotter from now on.

Example Sentences

1. Have you ever been to Hokkaido?
    ······Yes, once. I went there two years ago with some friends.

2. Have you ever ridden a horse?
    ······No, never, but I'd really like to.

3. What did you do during your winter holiday?
    ······I went to temples, shrines and other places in Kyoto, partied with my friends, and so on.

4. What do you want to do in Japan?
    ······I want to travel around, study the tea ceremony, and other things.

5. How are you feeling?
    ······Better, thank you.

6. You've got very good at Japanese, haven't you?
    ······Thank you, but I've still got a long way to go.

7. What you want to be when you grow up, Teresa?
    ······I want to be a doctor.

Conversation

I'll start dieting tomorrow

Everybody:	Cheers!
	···
Yoshiko Matsumoto:	You're not eating much, are you, Maria?
Maria:	No, I've been on a diet since yesterday.
Yoshiko Matsumoto:	I see. I've been on some diets, too.
Maria:	What sort of diets?
Yoshiko Matsumoto:	Like only eating apples every day, and drinking lots of water.
	But over-strict diets aren't good for you, are they?
Maria:	No, they aren't.
Yoshiko Matsumoto:	This ice cream very nice, Maria.
Maria:	Is it?
	...... OK, I'll start dieting again tomorrow.

III. Useful Words and Information

DENTŌ-BUNKA · GORAKU   Traditional Culture and Entertainment

sadō tea ceremony (ocha)	kadō flower arranging (ikebana)	shodō calligraphy
kabuki Kabuki	nō Noh	bunraku Bunraku
sumō sumo	jūdō judo	kendō kendo
karate karate	manzai·rakugo manzai, rakugo	igo·shōgi go, shogi
pachinko pachinko	karaoke karaoke	bon-odori Bon dance

121

19

IV. Grammar Notes

1. V ta-form

Forms of verbs ending in ta or da are called their ta-form. A verb's ta-form is created by changing the te or de of its te-form to ta or da respectively. (See Exercise A1, Lesson 19 of Main Text.)

te-form → ta-form

kaite → kaita

nonde → nonda

tabete → tabeta

kite → kita

shite → shita

2. | V ta-form **koto ga arimasu** | have the experience of V-ing

This sentence pattern is used to say that one has had a particular experience, without saying when that experience occurred.

① Uma ni notta koto ga arimasu.　　　　I've ridden a horse.

Note that the past tense is used when simply mentioning something that happened in the past.

② Kyonen Hokkaidō de uma ni norimashita.　I rode a horse last year in Hokkaido.

3. | V₁ **ta-form ri, V₂ ta-form ri shimasu** | V₁, V₂ and so on......

As already explained, the particle ya is used when citing two or more nouns as typical examples from a longer list. This sentence pattern is used when doing the same with verbs. The tense is shown at the end of the sentence.

③ Nichi-yōbi wa tenisu o shitari, eiga o mitari shimasu.

On Sundays, I play tennis, watch a film, and so on.

④ Nichi-yōbi wa tenisu o shitari, eiga o mitari shimashita.

Last Sunday, I played tennis, watched a film and did some other stuff.

[Note] Be sure not to confuse this sentence pattern with the V₁ te-form, [V₂ te-form,] V₃ sentence pattern presented in Lesson 16, which is used to enumerate all the members of a list of two or more successive actions in their order of occurrence.

⑤ Nichi-yōbi wa tenisu o shite, eiga o mimashita.

On Sunday, I played tennis and then watched a film.

Unlike with this sentence pattern, V₁ ta-form ri, V₂ ta-form ri shimasu is used to enumerate a few typical actions from a longer list, indicating no time relationship between them. Because it is used to list actions non-exhaustively, it would be unnatural to use it for mentioning actions that everyone usually does every day, such as getting up in the morning, eating meals, and going to bed at night.

4.

i-adj (～ ἴ) → ～ ku	
na-adj [ná] → ～ ni	narimasu
N ni	

become......

Narimasu indicates a change of state.

⑥ samui → samuku narimasu   Get cold.

⑦ genki[na] → genki ni narimasu   Get better.

⑧ 25-sai → 25-sai ni narimasu   Turn 25 [years old].

Lesson 20

I. Vocabulary

irimasu I 　[biza ga 〜]	いります 　[ビザが〜]	need, require [a visa]
shirabemasu II	しらべます	check, investigate
shūri-shimasu III	しゅうりします	repair
boku	ぼく	I (an informal equivalent of watashi used by men)
kimi*	きみ	you (an informal equivalent of anata used to address people of equal or lower status)
-kun	〜くん	Mr. (an informal equivalent of -san used to address people of equal or lower status; also often appended to boys' names)
un	うん	yes (an informal equivalent of hai)
uun	ううん	no (an informal equivalent of iie)
kotoba	ことば	word, language
kimono	きもの	kimono (traditional Japanese attire)
biza	ビザ	visa
hajime	はじめ	the beginning
owari	おわり	the end of 〜, The End
kotchi*	こっち	this way, this place (an informal equivalent of kochira)
sotchi	そっち	that way, that place near the listener (an informal equivalent of sochira)
atchi*	あっち	that way, that place over there (an informal equivalent of achira)
dotchi	どっち	which one (of two things), which way, where (an informal equivalent of dochira)
minna de	みんなで	all together
〜 kedo	〜けど	〜, but (an informal equivalent of ga)
onaka ga ippai desu	おなかが いっぱいです	(I'm) full

124

20

〈Kaiwa〉

| yokattara | よかったら | if you like |
| iroiro | いろいろ | various |

II. Translation

Sentence Patterns

1. Mr. Santos didn't come to the party.
2. There are a lot of people in Tokyo.
3. The sea in Okinawa was beautiful.
4. It's my birthday today.

Example Sentences

1. Like some ice cream?
   ······Yes, I would.

2. Do you have any scissors there?
   ······No, I don't.

3. Did you meet Ms. Kimura yesterday?
   ······No, I didn't.

4. Is that curry good?
   ······Yes, it's spicy, but it tastes nice.

5. Shall we all go to Kyoto tomorrow?
   ······Yes, that sounds good.

6. What would you like to eat?
   ······I'm full up at the moment, so I don't want to eat anything.

7. You free?
   ······Yes, I am. What do you want?
   Lend us a hand for a moment.

8. Do you have a dictionary?
   ······No, I don't.

Conversation

Shall we go together?

Kobayashi: Are you going home for the summer holidays?
Thawaphon: No, although I'd like to......
Kobayashi: I see.
            Have you ever been up Mount Fuji, Thawaphon?
Thawaphon: No, I haven't.
Kobayashi: How about going together, then?
Thawaphon: OK. When?
Kobayashi: How about the beginning of August?
Thawaphon: Fine.
Kobayashi: OK, I'll check a few things out and give you a call.
Thawaphon: Thanks, I'll be waiting.

III. Useful Words and Information

HITO NO YOBI-KATA   How to Address People

In families, people tend to call each other from the viewpoint of the youngest of the family. For example, a parent calls his/her eldest son or daughter 'oniichan'(elder brother) or 'onēchan' (elder sister) , standing in the position of his/her younger sister or brother.

When parents talk in the presence of their children, the husband calls his wife 'okāsan' (Mother) or 'mama'(Mom), and the wife calls her husband 'otōsan'(Father) or 'papa' (Pop). This practice, however, has been changing recently.

In Japan, people tend to call each other by the names of their role in the group to which they belong. For example, at work, a subordinate calls his boss by his job title. In shops, shop assistants call their customers 'o-kyaku-sama' (Mr./Ms. Customer). Doctors are called 'sensei' by their patients.

20

IV. Grammar Notes

1. Polite style and plain style

The Japanese language has two styles of speech: polite style and plain style.

Polite style	Plain style
Ashita Tōkyō e ikimasu. I shall be going to Tokyo tomorrow.	Ashita Tōkyō e iku. I'm off to Tokyo tomorrow.
Mainichi isogashii desu. I'm busy every day.	Mainichi isogashii. I'm busy every day.
Sumō ga suki desu. I like sumo.	Sumō ga suki da. I like sumo.
Fujisan ni noboritai desu. I'd like to climb Mt Fuji.	Fujisan ni noboritai. I want to climb Mt Fuji.
Doitsu e itta koto ga arimasen. I've never been to Germany.	Doitsu e itta koto ga nai. I've never been to Germany.

The predicates used in polite-style sentences accompanied by desu or masu are called the polite form, while the predicates used in plain-style sentences are called the plain form. (See Exercise A1, Lesson 20 of Main Text.)

2. Proper use of the polite style or plain style

1) Conversation

The polite style is used when speaking to a person one has met for the first time, to someone of higher status, and even to people in a similar age group whom one does not know very well.

The plain style is used when talking to one's close friends, colleagues and family members.

Be careful not to use the plain style to the wrong person, as this would be discourteous.

2) Writing

The polite style is commonly used in writing letters, while the plain style is used when writing dissertations, reports, diaries and so on.

3. Conversation in the plain style

1) Questions in the plain style usually omit the particle ka from the end, being pronounced with a rising intonation instead, e.g. nomu (↗) or nonda (↗).

① Kōhii o nomu? (↗)   Want some coffee?
   ……Un, nomu. (↘)   ……Yeah, sure.

2) In noun and na-adj questions, da (the plain form of desu), is omitted. In an answer in the affirmative, ending the sentence with da could sound a bit harsh, so it is either omitted entirely or replaced by a sentence-ending particle to soften the reply.

②   Konban hima?   You free tonight?
     ······Un, hima/hima da/hima da yo.   ······Yes, I am. (used by men)
     ······Un, hima/hima yo/hima da yo.   ······Yes, I am. (used by women)
     ······Uun, hima ja nai.   ······No, I'm not.

3) In the plain style, certain particles are often omitted if the meaning of the sentence is evident from the context.

③   Gohan [o] taberu?   Would you like something to eat?

④   Ashita Kyōto [e] ikanai?   How about going to Kyoto tomorrow?

⑤   Kono ringo [wa] oishii ne.   These apples are nice, aren't they?

⑥   Soko ni hasami [ga] aru?   Are there any scissors there?

However, particles like de, ni, kara, made and to are not omitted because the meaning of the sentence would be unclear without them.

4) In the plain style, the i of the V te-form iru is also often dropped.

⑦   Jisho, motte [i]ru?   Have you got a dictionary?
     ······Un, motte [i]ru.   ······Yes, I have.
     ······Uun, motte [i]nai.   ······No, I haven't.

5) kedo

Kedo works in the same way as ga and is often used in conversation.

⑧   Sono karē [wa] oishii?   Is that curry good?
     ······Un, karai kedo, oishii.   Yes, it's spicy, but it's nice.

⑨   Sumō no chiketto [ga] aru kedo, issho ni ikanai?
     ······Ii ne.

I've got some tickets for the sumo. Would you like to go with me?
······That'd be great.

Lesson 21

I. Vocabulary

omoimasu I	おもいます	think
iimasu I	いいます	say
kachimasu I	かちます	win
makemasu II*	まけます	lose, be beaten
arimasu I	あります	[a festival] be held, take place
[o-matsuri ga 〜]	[おまつりが〜]	
yaku ni tachimasu I	やくに たちます	be useful
ugokimasu I	うごきます	move, work
yamemasu II	やめます	quit or retire from [a company], stop, give up
[kaisha o 〜]	[かいしゃを〜]	
ki o tsukemasu II	きを つけます	pay attention, take care
ryūgaku-shimasu III	りゅうがくします	study abroad
muda[na]	むだ[な]	wasteful
fuben[na]	ふべん[な]	inconvenient
sugoi	すごい	awful, great（expresses astonishment or admiration）
hontō	ほんとう	true
uso*	うそ	lie
jidōsha	じどうしゃ	car, automobile
kōtsū	こうつう	transport, traffic
bukka	ぶっか	[commodity] prices
hōsō	ほうそう	announcement, broadcast
nyūsu	ニュース	news
anime	アニメ	anime（Japanese animated film）
manga	マンガ	comic book
dezain	デザイン	design, artwork
yume	ゆめ	dream
tensai	てんさい	genius
shiai	しあい	game, match（〜 o shimasu：play a game/match）

iken	いけん	opinion
hanashi	はなし	talk, speech, what one says, story (〜 o shimasu：talk, tell a story)
chikyū	ちきゅう	earth
tsuki	つき	moon
saikin	さいきん	recently, these days
tabun	たぶん	probably, perhaps, maybe
kitto	きっと	surely, definitely
hontō ni	ほんとうに	really
sonnani	そんなに	not so (used with negatives)
〜 ni tsuite	〜に ついて	about 〜, concerning 〜

〈Kaiwa〉

Hisashiburi desu ne.	ひさしぶりですね。	It's been a long time [since we last met].
〜 demo nomimasen ka.	〜でも のみませんか。	How about drinking 〜 or something?
mochiron	もちろん	of course
Mō kaeranai to…….	もう かえらないと……。	I have to get home now......

....

Ainshutain	アインシュタイン	Albert Einstein (1879-1955)
Gagārin	ガガーリン	Yuri Alekseyevich Gagarin (1934-1968)
Garireo	ガリレオ	Galileo Galilei (1564-1642)
Kingu-bokushi	キングぼくし	Martin Luther King, Jr. (1929-1968)
Furankurin	フランクリン	Benjamin Franklin (1706-1790)
Kaguyahime	かぐやひめ	Princess Kaguya (heroine of the old Japanese folk tale 'Taketori Monogatari')
Tenjin-matsuri	てんじんまつり	Tenjin Festival (a festival in Osaka)
Yoshino-yama	よしのやま	Mt. Yoshino (a mountain in Nara Prefecture)
kangarū	カンガルー	kangaroo
Kyaputen Kukku	キャプテン・クック	Captain James Cook (1728-1779)
Yōnen	ヨーネン	a fictitious company

II. Translation

Sentence Patterns

1. I think it's going to rain tomorrow.
2. I told my Dad I want to go abroad to study.
3. I bet you're tired, aren't you?

Example Sentences

1. Where's Mr. Miller?
   ······I think he's probably already gone home.

2. Does Mr. Miller know about this news?
   ······No, I don't think he does.

3. Which is more important, your job or your family?
   ······I think they're both important.

4. What do you think of Japan?
   ······I think the prices are high.

5. Do you say grace before meals?
   ······No, we don't, but we do say, "Itadakimasu".

6. Princess Kaguya said, "I must go back home to the Moon." Then she went back to the Moon. The End.
   ······The End? Mummy, I want to go to the Moon, too.

7. Did you say anything in the meeting?
   ······Yes, I said there was a lot of wasteful copying.

8. There's a festival in Kyoto in July, isn't there?
   ······Yes, there is.

Conversation

I think so, too

Matsumoto: Hello, Mr. Santos. I haven't seen you for a while, have I?

Santos: Hi, Mr. Matsumoto. Are you well?

Matsumoto: Yes, thanks. Shall we go and have for a beer or something?

Santos: Good idea.
....

Santos: There's a soccer match between Japan and Brazil at ten o'clock tonight, isn't there?

Matsumoto: Oh, yes, so there is.
Which team do you think will win, Mr. Santos?

Santos: Brazil, of course!

Matsumoto: Well, maybe. But Japan has also gotten better lately.

Santos: Yes, I think so, too, but......
Oh, I have to get home now......

Matsumoto: Yes, let's go home, shall we?

III. Useful Words and Information

YAKUSHOKU-MEI   Positions in Society

kuni	nation	shushō (naikaku sōri-daijin)	prime minister
todōfuken	prefecture	chiji	governor
shi	city	shichō	city mayor
machi	town	chōchō	town mayor
mura	village	sonchō	village headman, chief of the village

daigaku	university	gakuchō	[university] president
kōtōgakkō	upper secondary (senior high) school		
chūgakkō	lower secondary (junior high) school	kōchō	[school] head teacher, principal
shōgakkō	primary (elementary) school		
yōchien	kindergarten	enchō	[kindergarten] head teacher, principal

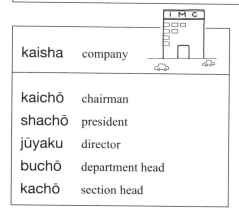

kaisha	company
kaichō	chairman
shachō	president
jūyaku	director
buchō	department head
kachō	section head

ginkō	bank
tōdori	[bank] president
shitenchō	branch manager

eki	station
ekichō	stationmaster

byōin	hospital
inchō	[hospital] director
buchō	department head
kangoshichō	head nurse

keisatsu	police station
shochō	officer in charge

IV. Grammar Notes

1. | **Plain form to omoimasu** | I think that......

The ideas or judgements expressed with omoimasu are indicated by the particle to. This sentence pattern is used in the following ways:

1) When expressing conjecture

   ①   Ashita ame ga furu to omoimasu.   I think it's going to rain tomorrow.

   ②   Terēza-chan wa mō neta to omoimasu.

        I think Teresa's already gone to bed.

To express a negative conjecture, the clause before to is put in the negative.

   ③   Mirā-san wa kono nyūsu o shitte imasu ka.

        ······Iie, shiranai to omoimasu.

        Has Mr. Miller heard that news?

        ······No, I don't think he has.

2) When stating an opinion

   ④   Nihon wa bukka ga takai to omoimasu.   I think that prices in Japan are high.

When asking someone's opinion about something, the expression ～ ni tsuite dō omoimasu ka is used, without putting to after the dō.

   ⑤   Atarashii kūkō ni tsuite dō omoimasu ka.

        ······Kirei desu ga, chotto kōtsū ga fuben da to omoimasu.

        What do you think of the new airport?

        ······I think it's lovely, but it's a bit hard to get to.

Agreement with someone else's opinion is expressed like this:

   ⑥   Kētai wa benri desu ne.   Mobile phones are handy, aren't they?

        ······Watashi mo sō omoimasu.   ······Yes, I think so, too.

2. | "Sentences" } **to iimasu** | say......
   | **Plain form** }

The particle to is used to report speech. There are two ways of doing this:

1) When reporting speech directly, it is repeated word for word. In writing, the words are placed inside double quotation marks " ".

   ⑦   Neru mae ni, "Oyasuminasai" to iimasu.

        We say, "Good night" before going to bed.

   ⑧   Mirā-san wa "Raishū Tōkyō e shutchō-shimasu" to iimashita.

        Mr. Miller said, "I'm going to Tokyo on business next week."

2) When reporting speech indirectly, the plain form is used before to.

   ⑨   Mirā-san wa Tōkyō e shutchō-suru to iimashita.

        Mr. Miller said that he would be going to Tokyo on business.

The tense of the quoted sentence is not affected by the tense of the main sentence.

The particle ni is used to indicate the person spoken to.

⑩ Chichi ni ryūgaku-shitai to iimashita.

I told my father that I wanted to study abroad.

3.

V	} plain form		
i-adj	}	**deshō?**	......right?
na-adj	} plain form		
N	} ~ dá		

This sentence form is used when seeking agreement or confirmation from the listener. deshō is spoken with a rising intonation.

The plain form is used before deshō, but without the ~ da in the case of a na-adj or noun.

⑪ Ashita pātii ni iku deshō?

You're going to the party tomorrow, right?

······Ē, ikimasu.   ······Yes, I am.

⑫ Hokkaidō wa samukatta deshō?   I bet it was cold in Hokkaido, wasn't it?

······Iie, sonnani samukunakatta desu.   ······No, it wasn't so cold.

4.   N₁ (place) de N₂ ga arimasu

When N₂ is a ceremony or event such as a party, concert, festival, incident or disaster, arimasu is used in the sense of 'to take place', 'to be held' or 'to occur'.

⑬ Tōkyō de Nihon to Burajiru no sakkā no shiai ga arimasu.

There's a soccer match between Japan and Brazil in Tokyo.

5.   N (occasion) de

The occasion at which an action takes place is marked by de.

⑭ Kaigi de nanika iken o iimashita ka.   Did you say anything at the meeting?

6.   N demo V

When recommending, suggesting, or expressing a hope for something, the particle demo is used to give an example, without restricting it to a specific one.

⑮ Chotto biiru demo nomimasen ka.   How about drinking a beer or something?

7.   V nai-form nai to······

This expression is created by omitting the ikemasen from V nai-form nai to ikemasen (see Lesson 17). V nai-form nai to ikemasen means more or less the same as V nai-form nakereba narimasen, which was presented in Lesson 17.

⑯ Mō kaeranai to······.   I have to be getting home......

135

Lesson 22

I. Vocabulary

kimasu II	きます	put on (a shirt, etc.)
hakimasu I	はきます	put on (shoes, trousers, etc.)
kaburimasu I	かぶります	put on (a hat, etc.)
kakemasu II	かけます	put on [glasses]
[megane o ～]	[めがねを～]	
shimasu III	します	put on [tie]
[nekutai o ～]	[ネクタイを～]	
umaremasu II	うまれます	be born
watashitachi	わたしたち	we
kōto	コート	coat
sētā	セーター	sweater
sūtsu*	スーツ	suit
bōshi	ぼうし	hat, cap
megane	めがね	glasses
kēki	ケーキ	cake
[o-]bentō	[お]べんとう	box lunch
robotto	ロボット	robot
yūmoa	ユーモア	humor
tsugō	つごう	convenience
yoku	よく	often

〈Renshū C〉

ēto	えーと	well, let me see
Omedetō [gozaimasu].	おめでとう ［ございます］。	Congratulations. (used on birthdays, at weddings, New Year's Day, etc.)

〈Kaiwa〉

O-sagashi desu ka.	おさがしですか。	Are you looking for ～ ?
dewa	では	Well then,
kochira	こちら	this (polite equivalent of kore)
yachin	やちん	rent
dainingu-kitchin	ダイニングキッチン	kitchen with a dining area
washitsu	わしつ	Japanese-style room
oshiire	おしいれ	Japanese-style closet
futon	ふとん	Japanese-style mattress and quilt

Pari	パリ	Paris
Banri no chōjō	ばんりの ちょうじょう	the Great Wall of China
Minna no ankēto	みんなの アンケート	title of a fictitious questionnaire

II. Translation

Sentence Patterns

1. This cake was made by Mr. Miller.
2. That person over there is Mr. Miller.
3. I've forgotten the words I learnt yesterday.
4. I don't have time to go shopping.

Example Sentences

1. These are some photographs I took at the Great Wall of China.
   ......Really? Amazing, isn't it?

2. Which is the painting that Karina did?
   ......That one. That painting of the sea.

3. Who's that person wearing a kimono?
   ......That's Ms. Kimura.

4. Mr. Yamada, where did you first meet your wife?
   ......At Osaka Castle.

5. How was the concert you went to with Ms. Kimura?
   ......It was very good.

6. What's the matter?
   ......I've lost the umbrella I bought yesterday.

7. What kind of house do you want?
   ......I want a house with a big garden.

8. Would you like to go and watch the soccer on Sunday?
   ......Sorry, I've promised to meet some friends on Sunday.

Conversation

What kind of flat are you looking for?

Letting agent: What kind of flat are you looking for?

Wang: Let me see......
A place where the rent is about eighty thousand yen, not far from the station, would be good.

Letting agent: How about this one, then?
It's ten minutes from the station, and the rent is eighty-three thousand yen.

Wang: It's got an eat-in kitchen and one Japanese-style room, right?
Excuse me. What's this?

Letting agent: That's an 'oshiire'. It's a place to put a futon in.

Wang: I see.
Can I see this flat today?

Letting agent: Yes. Shall we go now?

Wang: Yes, please.

III. Useful Words and Information

IFUKU　　Clothes

sūtsu suit	**wanpiisu** one-piece dress	**uwagi** jacket	**zubon/pantsu** trousers/pants **jiinzu** jeans
sukāto skirt	**burausu** blouse	**waishatsu** [white] shirt	**sētā** sweater
mafurā scarf, muffler **tebukuro**　gloves	**shitagi** underwear	**kutsushita**　socks **(pantii-)** **sutokkingu** tights, panty hose	**kimono**　kimono obi　obi
(ōbā-) kōto overcoat **rein-kōto** raincoat	**nekutai** tie, necktie **beruto**　belt	**haihiiru** high heels **būtsu** boots **undōgutsu** trainers, sneakers	**zōri**　　　**tabi** zori　　　tabi

IV. Grammar Notes

1. Noun modification

Lessons 2 and 8 explained how to modify nouns.

Mirā-san no uchi	Mr. Miller's house (See Lesson 2.)
atarashii uchi	a new house (See Lesson 8.)
kireina uchi	a beautiful house (See Lesson 8.)

The modifying word or clause comes before the noun. This lesson explains how to use a clause to modify a noun.

1) Verbs, adjectives and nouns in a clause that modifies a noun are in the plain form. With na-adjectives, this is ~ na, and with nouns it is ~ no.

① Kyōto e
- iku hito — a person who goes to Kyoto
- ikanai hito — a person who does not go to Kyoto
- itta hito — a person who went to Kyoto
- ikanakatta hito — a person who did not go to Kyoto

se ga takakute, kami ga kuroi hito	a tall, black-haired person
shinsetsu de kireina hito	a beautiful, kind person
65-sai no hito	a 65-year-old person

2) Noun-modifying clauses are used with the various sentence patterns illustrated below.

② Kore wa Mirā-san ga sunde ita uchi desu.
This is the house where Mr. Miller used to live.

③ Mirā-san ga sunde ita uchi wa furui desu.
The house where Mr. Miller used to live is old.

④ Mirā-san ga sunde ita uchi o kaimashita.
I bought the house where Mr. Miller used to live.

⑤ Watashi wa Mirā-san ga sunde ita uchi ga suki desu.
I like the house where Mr. Miller used to live.

⑥ Mirā-san ga sunde ita uchi ni neko ga imashita.
There was a cat in the house where Mr. Miller used to live.

⑦ Mirā-san ga sunde ita uchi e itta koto ga arimasu.
I've been to the house where Mr. Miller used to live.

3) The subject of a noun-modifying clause is marked by ga.

⑧ Kore wa Mirā-san ga tsukutta kēki desu.
    This cake was baked by Mr. Miller.

⑨ Watashi wa Karina-san ga kaita e ga suki desu.
    I like the picture that Karina painted.

⑩ [Anata wa] kare ga umareta tokoro o shitte imasu ka.
    Do you know the place where he was born?

2. | V-dictionary form jikan/yakusoku/yōji |

When talking about the time required for doing something or describing an appointment, errand, etc., the verb is put in the dictionary form and is placed in front of the noun jikan, yakusoku, yōji, etc.

⑪ Watashi wa asagohan o taberu jikan ga arimasen.
    I don't have time to eat breakfast.

⑫ Watashi wa tomodachi to eiga o miru yakusoku ga arimasu.
    I've arranged to see a film with some friends.

⑬ Kyō wa shiyakusho e iku yōji ga arimasu.
    I have to do something at City Hall today.

3. | V masu-form mashō ka | Shall we......?

This sentence pattern was presented in Lesson 14 as an expression for when the speaker is offering to do something for the listener. However, in this Lesson's Conversation, it is presented as an expression for when the speaker is suggesting to the listener that they do something together.

⑭ Kono heya, kyō miru koto ga dekimasu ka. Can I see this flat today?
    ······Ē. Ima kara ikimashō ka.   ······Yes. Shall we go now?

141

Lesson 23

I. Vocabulary

kikimasu I	ききます	ask [the teacher]
[sensei ni 〜]	[せんせいに〜]	
mawashimasu I	まわします	turn
hikimasu I	ひきます	pull
kaemasu II	かえます	change
sawarimasu I	さわります	touch [a door]
[doa ni 〜]	[ドアに〜]	
demasu II	でます	[change] come out
[otsuri ga 〜]	[おつりが〜]	
arukimasu I	あるきます	walk
watarimasu I	わたります	cross [a bridge]
[hashi o 〜]	[はしを〜]	
magarimasu I	まがります	turn [to the right]
[migi e 〜]	[みぎへ〜]	
sabishii	さびしい	lonely
[o-]yu	[お]ゆ	hot water
oto	おと	sound
saizu	サイズ	size
koshō	こしょう	breakdown (-shimasu : break down)
michi	みち	road, way
kōsaten	こうさてん	crossroads
shingō	しんごう	traffic lights
kado	かど	corner
hashi	はし	bridge
chūshajō	ちゅうしゃじょう	car park, parking lot
tatemono	たてもの	building
nankai mo	なんかいも	many times
-me	一め	the -th (indicating order)

Shōtokutaishi	しょうとくたいし	Prince Shotoku (574-622)
Hōryūji	ほうりゅうじ	Horyuji Temple, a temple in Nara Prefecture built by Prince Shotoku at the beginning of the 7th century
Genki-cha	げんきちゃ	a fictitious tea
Honda-eki	ほんだえき	a fictitious station
Toshokan-mae	としょかんまえ	a fictitious bus stop

23

II. Translation

Sentence Patterns

1. When you borrow a book from the library, you need your card.
2. If you press this button, your change comes out.

Example Sentences

1. Do you watch much TV?
   ······Well, I usually watch baseball games when they're on.

2. What do you do when there's nothing in the fridge?
   ······I go and eat in a nearby restaurant.

3. Did you switch off the air conditioner when you left the meeting room?
   ······Yes, I did.

4. Where do you buy your clothes and shoes, Mr. Santos?
   ······I buy them when I go back to my own country, because Japanese ones are too small.

5. What's that?
   ······It's 'Genki-cha'. I drink it when I don't feel very well.

6. Won't you come and visit us when you have some time to spare?
   ······Yes, I will. Thank you.

7. Did you have any part-time jobs when you were at university?
   ······Yes, sometimes.

8. There's no hot water coming out.
   ······It'll come out if you press there.

9. Excuse me, where's the city hall?
   ······Go straight down this street, and it's on the left. It's an old building.

Conversation

How do you get there?

Librarian: Hello, Midori Library.

Karina: Can you tell me how to get to you, please?

Librarian: Get on the number twelve bus at Honda station and get off at Toshokanmae.
It's the third stop.

Karina: The third stop, right?

Librarian: Yes, when you get off, you'll see a park in front of you.
The library is the white building in the park.

Karina: I see.
And what do I need to bring with me to take out a book?

Librarian: Please bring something that shows your name and address.

Karina: OK. Thank you very much.

III. Useful Words and Information

DŌRO · KŌTSŪ   Roads and Traffic

① hodō — pavement, sidewalk
② shadō — road
③ kōsoku-dōro — motorway, expressway
④ tōri — street
⑤ kōsaten — crossing
⑥ ōdan-hodō — pedestrian crossing
⑦ hodōkyō — pedestrian bridge
⑧ kado — corner

⑨ shingō — traffic light
⑩ saka — slope
⑪ fumikiri — railway crossing
⑫ gasorin-sutando — petrol station, gas station

23

145

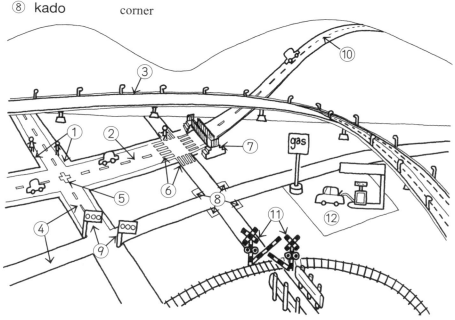

tomare	shinnyū-kinshi	ippō-tsūkō	chūsha-kinshi	usetsu-kinshi
Stop	No Entry	One Way	No Parking	No Right Turn

IV. Grammar Notes

1.

| V-dictionary form
 V nai-form nai <br> i-adj (～ i)
 na-adj na
 N no } toki, ～ (main clause) | When...... |

Toki is used to connects two sentences while expressing a time or occasion when the state or action described in the main sentence exists or occurs. The form of the word preceding toki is the same as the form that modifies a noun.

① Toshokan de hon o kariru toki, kādo ga irimasu.
  You need your card when you borrow a book from the library.

② Tsukai-kata ga wakaranai toki, watashi ni kiite kudasai.
  If you don't know how to use it, please ask me.

③ Karada no chōshi ga warui toki, "Genki-cha" o nomimasu.
  When I don't feel very well, I drink 'Genki-cha'.

④ Himana toki, uchi e asobi ni kimasen ka.
  Please come and visit me when you have some free time.

⑤ Tsuma ga byōki no toki, kaisha o yasumimasu.
  I take time off when my wife is ill.

⑥ Wakai toki, amari benkyō-shimasendeshita.
  I didn't study very much when I was young.

⑦ Kodomo no toki, yoku kawa de oyogimashita.
  I often swam in the river when I was a child.

The tense of the clause modifying toki is not affected by the tense of the main clause.

2.

| V-dictionary form
 V ta-form } toki, ～ (main clause) | When...... |

When the verb in front of toki is in the dictionary form, whatever is described in the main clause happened before whatever is described in the ～ toki clause. When the verb in front of toki is in the ta-form, whatever is described in the main clause happened after whatever is described in the ～ toki clause.

⑧ Pari e iku toki, kaban o kaimashita.
  I bought a bag when going to Paris.

⑨ Pari e itta toki, kaban o kaimashita.
  I bought a bag when I went to Paris.

⑧ means that the bag was bought before arriving in Paris, i.e. it was bought on the way there, while ⑨ means that the bag was bought after arriving in Paris, i.e. it was bought in Paris.

3. | **V-dictionary form to, ～ (main clause)** | If ...... then ......

This sentence pattern is used to indicate that if a certain action, situation or phenomenon (the one before *to*) occurs, then another action, situation or phenomenon (the one in the main clause, after *to*) will inevitably occur.

⑩　Kono botan o osu to, otsuri ga demasu.
　　If you press this button, you'll get your change.

⑪　Kore o mawasu to, oto ga ōkiku narimasu.
　　When you turn this, it gets louder.

⑫　Migi e magaru to, yūbinkyoku ga arimasu.
　　If you turn right, you'll see a post office.

4. | **N ga adj**

It was explained in Lesson 14 that *ga* is used when describing a phenomenon in terms of how it was perceived with the five senses (sight, hearing, etc.) or when objectively reporting an event. *Ga* can be used not only with verb sentences but also with adjective sentences.

⑬　Oto ga chiisai desu.　　　　The volume is low.

5. | **N o motionV**

O is used with motion verbs such as sanpo-shimasu, watarimasu and arukimasu to indicate the place that people or things pass through.

⑭　Kōen o sanpo-shimasu.　　　I go for a walk in the park. (See Lesson 13.)

⑮　Michi o watarimasu.　　　　I cross the road.

⑯　Kōsaten o migi e magarimasu.　　I turn right at the intersection.

Lesson 24

I. Vocabulary

kuremasu	II	くれます	give (me)
naoshimasu	I	なおします	repair, correct
tsurete ikimasu	I	つれて いきます	take (someone)
tsurete kimasu	III *	つれて きます	bring (someone)
okurimasu	I	おくります	escort [someone], go with
[hito o ～]		[ひとを～]	
shōkai-shimasu	III	しょうかいします	introduce
annai-shimasu	III	あんないします	show around, show the way
setsumei-shimasu	III	せつめいします	explain
ojiisan/		おじいさん／	grandfather, old man
ojiichan		おじいちゃん	
obāsan/		おばあさん／	grandmother, old woman
obāchan		おばあちゃん	
junbi		じゅんび	preparation（～[o] -shimasu：prepare）
hikkoshi		ひっこし	moving out（～[o] -shimasu：move out）
[o-]kashi		[お]かし	sweets, snacks
hōmusutei		ホームステイ	homestay
zenbu		ぜんぶ	all
jibun de		じぶんで	by oneself

〈Kaiwa〉

hoka ni	ほかに	besides

....

Haha no hi	ははの ひ	Mother's Day

24

II. Translation

Sentence Patterns

1. Ms. Sato gave me some chocolate.
2. Mr. Yamada corrected my report for me.
3. My mother sent me a sweater.
4. I lent Ms. Kimura a book.

Example Sentences

1. Do you love Granny, Taro?
   ······Yes, I do. She always gives me sweet things to eat.

2. Nice wine, isn't it?
   ······Yes, Ms. Sato gave it to me. It's French.

3. Mr. Miller, did you cook all the food at yesterday's party yourself?
   ······No, Mr. Wang helped me.

4. Did you go by train?
   ······No, Mr. Yamada took me in his car.

5. Taro, what are you going to do for your mother on Mother's Day?
   ······I'm going to play the piano for her.

Conversation

Shall I come and help?

Karina: Mr. Wang, you're moving on Sunday, aren't you?
Shall I come and help?

Wang: Thank you.
OK then, if you don't mind, please come at about nine o'clock.

Karina: Is anyone else coming to help?

Wang: Mr. Yamada and Mr. Miller are coming.

Karina: What about a car?

Wang: Mr. Yamada is lending me his.

Karina: What are you doing about lunch?

Wang: Er······

Karina: Shall I bring a packed lunch?

Wang. Yes, please. Thanks.

Karina: See you on Sunday then.

III. Useful Words and Information

ZŌTŌ NO SHŪKAN   Exchanging Gifts

otoshidama	Small gift of money given by parents and relatives to children on New Year's Day
nyūgaku-iwai	Gift celebrating admission to school (money, stationery, book, etc.)
sotsugyō-iwai	Graduation gift (money, stationery, book, etc.)
kekkon-iwai	Wedding gift (money, household goods, etc.)
shussan-iwai	Gift celebrating a birth (baby clothes, toys, etc.)
o-chūgen [Jul. or Aug.] o-seibo [Dec.]	Gift for a person whose care you are under, e.g., doctor, teacher, boss, etc. (food, etc.)
o-kōden	Condolence money
o-mimai	Present given when visiting a sick or injured person (flowers, fruit, etc.)

Noshibukuro   Special decorated envelope for money gifts

The right envelope for the occasion should be used.

For weddings (with red and white, or gold and silver ribbon)

For celebrations other than weddings (with red and white, or gold and silver ribbon)

For funerals (with black and white ribbon)

IV. Grammar Notes

1. kuremasu

The word agemasu (give), which was taught in Lesson 7, cannot be used to talk about someone else giving something to the speaker or a member of his or her family. In that case, the word kuremasu is used.

① Watashi wa Satō-san ni hana o agemashita.

    I gave some flowers to Ms. Sato.

    ✗ Satō-san wa watashi ni Kurisumasu-kādo o agemashita.

② Satō-san wa watashi ni Kurisumasu-kādo o kuremashita.
    Ms. Sato gave me a Christmas card.

③ Satō-san wa imōto ni o-kashi o kuremashita.
    Ms. Sato gave some candies to my younger sister.

2.

V te-form	agemasu
	moraimasu
	kuremasu

Agemasu, moraimasu and kuremasu refer to the giving and receiving of things, while -te agemasu, -te moraimasu and -te kuremasu are used to denote that an action confers some kind of profit or benefit on the recipient.

1) | V te-form agemasu |

The pattern verb te-form agemasu is used when the person doing the action is taken as the subject. It shows that the action confers some kind of profit or benefit on the recipient.

④ Watashi wa Kimura-san ni hon o kashite agemashita.
    I lent Ms. Kimura a book.

Because the -te agemasu pattern denotes the conferral of some kind of profit or benefit, it could sound patronizing if used when the recipient is of higher status than the person conferring the profit or benefit. It is better in this case to use the pattern verb masu-form mashō ka (see Lesson 14-5).

⑤ Takushii o yobimashō ka.
    Shall I call a cab? (See Lesson 14.)

⑥ Tetsudaimashō ka.
    May I help you? (See Lesson 14.)

2) | V te-form moraimasu |

⑦ Watashi wa Yamada-san ni toshokan no denwa-bangō o oshiete moraimashita.
    Mr. Yamada told me the telephone number of the library.

This shows that the speaker feels that the person for whom the action was performed (who is taken as the subject of this sentence) has received some profit or benefit from the action. When the subject is watashi, it is usually omitted.

3) | Verb te-form kuremasu |

⑧ Haha wa [watashi ni] sētā o okutte kuremashita.

My mother sent me a sweater.

Here, the person performing the action is taken as the subject, and the form shows that the speaker feels that the person for whom the action was performed has benefited from the action. When the person benefiting from the action (marked by the particle ni) is watashi, it is usually omitted.

[Note] In a sentence using -te agemasu or -te kuremasu, the particle that marks the person receiving the benefit is the same as in an equivalent sentence that does not use -te agemasu or -te kuremasu.

Watashi ni ryokō no shashin o misemasu.

↓

Watashi ni ryokō no shashin o misete kuremasu.

He shows me the photos taken during the travel.

Watashi o Ōsakajō e tsurete ikimasu.

↓

Watashi o Ōsakajō e tsurete itte kuremasu.

He takes me to Osaka Castle.

Watashi no hikkoshi o tetsudaimasu.

↓

Watashi no hikkoshi o tetsudatte kuremasu.

He helps me move.

3. | N₁ wa N₂ ga V |

⑨ Oishii wain desu ne.

······Ē, [kono wain wa] Satō-san ga kuremashita.

This wine is very nice, isn't it?

······Yes, Ms. Sato gave it to me.

The response to this question takes as its topic the object of the sentence Satō-san ga kono wain o kuremashita, i.e. kono wain o (see Lesson 17-5). Since kono wain wa is understood by both the speaker and the listener, it can be omitted. As the subject of this sentence is Satō-san, it is marked by ga.

Lesson 25

I. Vocabulary

kangaemasu II	かんがえます	think, consider
tsukimasu I	つきます	arrive
torimasu I	とります	grow old
[toshi o 〜]	[としを〜]	
tarimasu II	たります	be enough, be sufficient
inaka	いなか	countryside, hometown
chansu	チャンス	chance
oku	おく	hundred million
moshi [-tara]	もし [〜たら]	if
imi	いみ	meaning

〈**Renshū C**〉

moshi moshi	もしもし	hello (used on the phone)

〈**Kaiwa**〉

tenkin	てんきん	transfer (-shimasu：be transferred to another office)
koto	こと	thing, matter (〜 no koto：thing about 〜)
hima	ひま	free time
[Iroiro] osewa ni narimashita.	[いろいろ] おせわに なりました。	Thank you for everything you've done for me.
ganbarimasu Ⅰ	がんばります	do one's best
Dōzo o-genki de.	どうぞ おげんきで。	Please take care of youreslf. (said when expecting a long separation)

....

Betonamu	ベトナム	Vietnam

25

155

II. Translation

Sentence Patterns

1. I'm not going out if it rains.
2. I'm going out even if it rains.

Example Sentences

1. What would you like to do if you had a hundred million yen?
   ⋯⋯ I'd like to build a school.

2. What will you do if there aren't any trains or buses running?
   ⋯⋯ I'll walk home.

3. That new shoe shop has a lot of nice shoes, you know.
   ⋯⋯ Really? I'd like to buy a pair if they're cheap enough.

4. Do I have to come tomorrow, too?
   ⋯⋯ No, if you can't make it, please come next week.

5. Have you thought of a name for the baby yet?
   ⋯⋯ Yes, Hikaru if it's a boy, and Aya if it's a girl.

6. Are you going to get a job as soon as you've left university?
   ⋯⋯ No, I want to go travelling around the world for a year or so.

7. Miss, I don't know what this word means.
   ⋯⋯ Did you look it up in the dictionary?
   Yes, but I still don't understand it.

8. Do you put the air conditioner on when it's hot?
   ⋯⋯ No, I don't put it on even if it's hot. I don't think it's good for one's health.

Conversation

Thanks for everything

Kimura: Congratulations on your move.

Miller: Thank you.

Kimura: We'll miss you, Mr. Miller when you've gone to Tokyo, won't we?

Sato: Yes, we will.

Kimura: Even after you've gone to Tokyo, please don't forget Osaka, will you?

Miller: Of course not. Everybody, when you have some spare time, please be sure to come and visit me in Tokyo.

Santos: And you please call us if you come to Osaka, Mr. Miller, and let's go out for a drink together.

Miller: Yes, definitely.
Everybody, I'm really grateful for everything you've done for me.

Sato: Good luck, and look after yourself.

Miller: Yes, I will. And all of you take care, too.

25

156

III. Useful Words and Information

HITO NO ISSHŌ Life

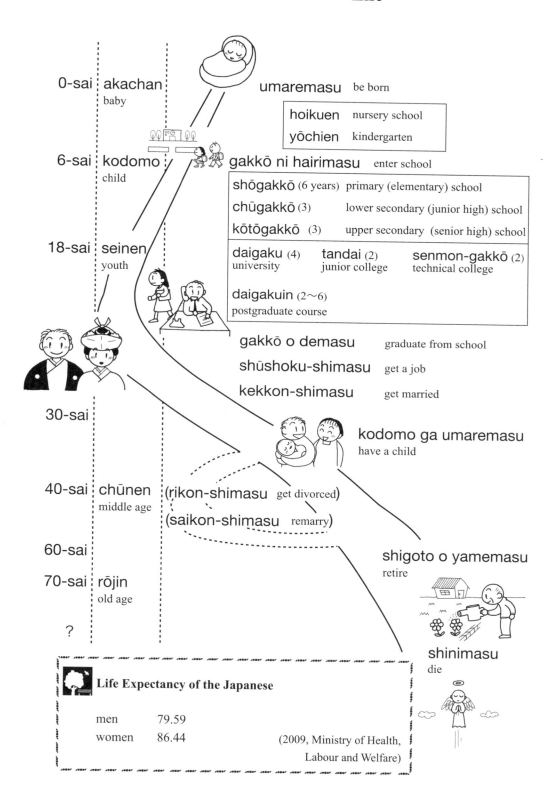

0-sai | akachan
baby

umaremasu be born

hoikuen   nursery school

yōchien   kindergarten

6-sai | kodomo
child

gakkō ni hairimasu   enter school

shōgakkō (6 years) primary (elementary) school

chūgakkō (3)   lower secondary (junior high) school

kōtōgakkō (3)   upper secondary (senior high) school

18-sai | seinen
youth

daigaku (4)   tandai (2)   senmon-gakkō (2)
university   junior college   technical college

daigakuin (2〜6)
postgraduate course

gakkō o demasu   graduate from school

shūshoku-shimasu   get a job

kekkon-shimasu   get married

30-sai

kodomo ga umaremasu
have a child

40-sai | chūnen
middle age

(rikon-shimasu get divorced)

(saikon-shimasu remarry)

60-sai

shigoto o yamemasu
retire

70-sai | rōjin
old age

?

shinimasu
die

Life Expectancy of the Japanese

men   79.59
women   86.44

(2009, Ministry of Health,
Labour and Welfare)

25

IV. Grammar Notes

1. | **Plain past form ra, ~ (main clause)** | If......

Attaching ra to the past-tense plain form of verbs, adjectives, or nouns, makes there conditional. The clause that follows it (the main clause) describes what will happen if the conditional clause were true. The speaker's opinion, wishes, invitations, requests, etc. can be expressed in the main clause.

① Okane ga attara, ryokō-shimasu.

    If I had some money, I'd go travelling.

② Jikan ga nakattara, terebi o mimasen.
    If I don't have time, I won't watch TV.

③ Yasukattara, pasokon o kaitai desu.
    I'd like to buy a PC if I can find a cheap one.

④ Hima dattara, tetsudatte kudasai.
    Please lend me a hand if you're free.

⑤ Ii tenki dattara, sanpo-shimasen ka.
    Shall we go for a walk if the weather's nice?

[Note] Expressions of wish, desire, invitation, request and so on cannot be used in a clause (the main clause) following ~ to.

                     ┌konsāto ni ikimasu.   (intention)

                     ├konsāto ni ikitai desu.   (wish)

× Jikan ga aru to,

                     ├konsāto ni ikimasen ka. (invitation)

                     └chotto tetsudatte kudasai. (request)

2. | **V ta-form ra, ~ (main clause)** | When....../After....../Once......

This pattern is used to express that a certain action will be done or a certain situation will arise on the completion or occurrence of a matter, action or state that the speaker is certain will happen.

⑥ 10-ji ni nattara, dekakemashō.
    Shall we go out once it gets to 10 o'clock?

⑦ Uchi e kaettara, sugu shawā o abimasu.
    I take a shower as soon as I get home.

3.

| V te-form
V nai-form nakute
i-adj (~*i*) →~ kute
na-adj [*na*] →~ de
N de | } mo, ~ (main clause) | Even if...... |

This expression is used to present contrasting conditions. The clause that follows te-form mo (the main clause) describes something that will happen that would not normally be expected to happen if what was stated in the main clause were true.

⑧   Ame ga futte mo, sentaku-shimasu.   I'll do the laundry even if it rains.

⑨   Yasukute mo, watashi wa gurūpu-ryokō ga kirai desu.
    I hate package holidays, even if they are cheap.

⑩   Benri de mo, pasokon o tsukaimasen.
    I'm not going to use a PC, even if it is convenient.

⑪   Nichi-yōbi de mo, hatarakimasu.   I'm going to work, even if it is Sunday.

4.   **moshi**

Moshi is used in conjunction with -tara to give notice that the clause following it is conditional. It intensifies the speaker's sense of conditionality.

⑫   Moshi 1-oku-en attara, iroirona kuni o ryokō-shitai desu.
    If I had a hundred million yen, I'd like to travel round the world.

5.   Subject of a subordinate clause

It was explained in Lesson 16-2 that the subject of the clause -te kara is marked by ga. In the same way as -te kara, ~ toki, ~ to, ~ mae ni, etc., the subject of a subordinate clause containing -tara or -te mo is also marked by ga.

⑬   Tomodachi ga kuru mae ni, heya o sōji-shimasu.
    I'm going to clean up my room before my friends arrive. (See Lesson 18.)

⑭   Tsuma ga byōki no toki, kaisha o yasumimasu.
    I take time off when my wife is ill. (See Lesson 23.)

⑮   Tomodachi ga yakusoku no jikan ni konakattara, dō shimasu ka.
    What will you do if your friends don't arrive at the agreed time? (See Lesson 25.)

25

159

Article 1: **Topic and Subject**

....

1. What is a Topic?

    Most Japanese sentences have a topic. The topic appears at the head of the sentence and indicates what is being discussed in the sentence. Sentence (1) below, for example, establishes Tōkyō as the topic and then discusses it, stating that it is Nihon no shuto.

(1) <u>Tōkyō wa</u> Nihon no shuto desu.   Tokyo is the capital of Japan.

    Similarly, sentences (2) and (3) below discuss the topics kono heya and watashi respectively.

(2) <u>Kono heya wa</u> shizuka desu.   This room is quiet.

(3) <u>Watashi wa</u> senshū Dizuniirando e ikimashita.

   I went to Disneyland last week.

    The topic of a sentence is marked by the particle wa. This means that a sentence with a topic is composed of two main parts, one before the wa (the topic) and the other after it (the discourse).

(1) <u>Tōkyō wa</u> Nihon no shuto desu.
     topic   discourse

2. What is a Subject?

    The subject of a sentence is the most important element for the sentence's predicate (a verb, adjective or noun + desu). For example, with verbs such as nomimasu (drink) or hashirimasu (run), the subject is whoever is doing the drinking or running; with verbs such as imasu or arimasu (be, exist), it is the person or thing that exists; with verbs such as furimasu (rain) or fukimasu (blow) it is the event's principal actor (i.e. whatever is raining or blowing); with adjectives such as ōkii desu (big) or yūmei desu (famous) or nouns such as gakusei desu (student) or byōki desu (illness), it is the possessor of the attribute mentioned; and with adjectival predicates such as suki desu (like) or kowai desu (fear), it is the experiencer of the feeling mentioned. Thus, all of the noun phrases underlined in the examples below are subjects.

    In sentences that do not have a topic, the subject is marked by the particle ga.

(4) <u>Tarō ga</u> biiru o nomimashita.   Taro drank some beer.

(5) Tsukue no ue ni <u>hon ga</u> arimasu.   There is a book on the desk.

(6) Kinō <u>ame ga</u> furimashita.   It rained yesterday.

3. How Do Topics and Subjects Relate to Each Other?

　　Although topics and subjects are different concepts, they are closely related. In most sentences with a topic, the topic is also the subject. For example, Tanaka-san, Satō-san and watashi in sentences (7), (8) and (9) below are all topics (because they are all marked with wa), but at the same time they are also subjects (because they are each the possessor of an attribute or the experiencer of a feeling).

(7) <u>Tanaka-san wa</u> yūmei desu.   Mr. Tanaka is famous.

(8) <u>Satō-san wa</u> gakusei desu.   Ms. Sato is a student.

(9) <u>Watashi wa</u> inu ga kowai desu.   I'm scared of dogs.

　　Although it is relatively common for the topic and subject of a sentence to coincide like this, sometimes they do not. In sentence (10) below, for example, kono hon is the topic (because it is marked with wa), but (because it is Tanaka-san who performs the action of kakimasu) kono hon is not the subject.

(10) <u>Kono hon wa</u> Tanaka-san ga kakimashita.   Mr. Tanaka wrote this book.

　　Sentence (10) can be thought of as being sentence (11) with kono hon o taken as the topic.

(11) Tanaka-san ga <u>kono hon o</u> kakimashita.   Mr. Tanaka wrote this book.

(12) <u>Kono hon o̶ wa</u> Tanaka-san ga kakimashita.   Mr. Tanaka wrote this book.

In other words, kono hon has moved to the head of the sentence, and is marked with wa to indicate that it is the topic. However, because o and wa cannot be used together when this is done, o is eliminated and only wa remains, forming sentence (10).

　　Note that, although ga and o cannot be combined with wa, other particles can, so sentences like (13) and (14) are possible.

(13) <u>Tanaka-san ni wa</u> watashi ga renraku-shimasu.

　　I will get in touch with Mr. Tanaka.

(14) <u>Yamada-san kara wa</u> henji ga kimasendeshita.

　　No reply came from Ms. Yamada.

4. Sentences with and without Topics

　　Although most Japanese sentences have topics, some do not. In a sentence with a topic, the subject is marked by wa, and in a sentence without a topic, it is marked by ga. Some examples of the use of topic-less sentences are given below.

1) When describing an event exactly as seen, heard, etc.

A sentence without a topic is used when describing an event exactly as perceived by any of the five senses:

(15) A, <u>ame ga</u> futte imasu.   Oh, it's raining.

(16) Rajio no <u>oto ga</u> chiisai desu.   The radio's [too] quiet.

(17) (mado no soto o mite) <u>Tsuki ga</u> kirei da nā.

(looking out of a window) The moon's lovely, isn't it?

2) When communicating an event objectively, or at the start of a story

A topic-less sentence is also used in these cases:

(18) Kinō <u>Tarō ga</u> kimashita.   Taro came yesterday.

(19) Raishū <u>pātii ga</u> arimasu.   There's a party next week.

(20) Mukashi mukashi aru tokoro ni <u>ojiisan to obāsan ga</u> imashita.

Long, long ago, in a certain place, there was an old man and an old woman.

Article 2: **Clauses**

....

A clause is the form that a sentence takes when it is part of a longer sentence.

For example, in (1) and (2) below, the sentences Tanaka-san ga koko e kimashita and ashita ame ga furimasu have become part of a longer sentence, taking the underlined forms.

(1) <u>Tanaka-san ga koko e kita toki</u>, Yamada-san wa imasendeshita.

When Ms. Tanaka arrived, Mr. Yamada wasn't here.

(2) <u>Ashita ame ga futtara</u>, watashi wa dekakemasen.

If it rains tomorrow, I'm not going out.

A clause that forms part of a longer sentence in this way is called a subordinate clause, while the part of the sentence left behind if the subordinate clause is removed is called the main clause.

A subordinate clause amplifies the meaning of the main clause. For example, the subordinate clause in example (2) limits what is said in the main clause by specifying ashita ame ga futtara as a condition of my not going out.

In Japanese, a subordinate clause usually precedes the main clause.

The subject of a subordinate clause is marked by ga, not by wa, except when the clause is a ～ ga or a ～ kedo clauses.

APPENDICES

I . Numerals

0	zero, rei	100	hyaku
1	ichi	200	ni-hyaku
2	ni	300	san-byaku
3	san	400	yon-hyaku
4	yon, shi	500	go-hyaku
5	go	600	rop-pyaku
6	roku	700	nana-hyaku
7	nana, shichi	800	hap-pyaku
8	hachi	900	kyū-hyaku
9	kyū, ku		
10	jū	1,000	sen
11	jū ichi	2,000	ni-sen
12	jū ni	3,000	san-zen
13	jū san	4,000	yon-sen
14	jū yon, jū shi	5,000	go-sen
15	jū go	6,000	roku-sen
16	jū roku	7,000	nana-sen
17	jū nana, jū shichi	8,000	has-sen
18	jū hachi	9,000	kyū-sen
19	jū kyū, jū ku		
20	ni-jū	10,000	ichi-man
30	san-jū	100,000	jū-man
40	yon-jū	1,000,000	hyaku-man
50	go-jū	10,000,000	sen-man
60	roku-jū	100,000,000	ichi-oku
70	nana-jū, shichi-jū		
80	hachi-jū	17.5	jū nana ten go
90	kyū-jū	0.83	rei ten hachi san

$\frac{1}{2}$ ni-bun no ichi

$\frac{3}{4}$ yon-bun no san

II. Expressions of time

day	morning	night
ototoi the day before yesterday	ototoi no asa the morning before last	ototoi no ban (yoru) the night before last
kinō yesterday	kinō no asa yesterday morning	kinō no ban (yoru) last night
kyō today	kesa this morning	konban (kyō no yoru) tonight
ashita tomorrow	ashita no asa tomorrow morning	ashita no ban (yoru) tomorrow night
asatte the day after tomorrow	asatte no asa the morning after next	asatte no ban (yoru) the night after next
mainichi every day	maiasa every morning	maiban every night

week	month	year
sensenshū (ni-shūkan mae) the week before last	sensengetsu (ni-kagetsu mae) the month before last	ototoshi the year before last
senshū last week	sengetsu last month	kyonen last year
konshū this week	kongetsu this month	kotoshi this year
raishū next week	raigetsu next month	rainen next year
saraishū the week after next	saraigetsu the month after next	sarainen the year after next
maishū every week	maitsuki every month	maitoshi, mainen every year

Telling time

o'clock -ji		minute -fun/-pun	
1	ichi-ji	1	ip-pun
2	ni-ji	2	ni-fun
3	san-ji	3	san-pun
4	yo-ji	4	yon-pun
5	go-ji	5	go-fun
6	roku-ji	6	rop-pun
7	shichi-ji	7	nana-fun
8	hachi-ji	8	hap-pun
9	ku-ji	9	kyū-fun
10	jū-ji	10	jup-pun, jip-pun
11	jū ichi-ji	15	jū go-fun
12	jū ni-ji	30	san-jup-pun, san-jip-pun, han
?	nan-ji	?	nan-pun

the days of the week -yōbi	
nichi-yōbi	Sunday
getsu-yōbi	Monday
ka-yōbi	Tuesday
sui-yōbi	Wednesday
moku-yōbi	Thursday
kin-yōbi	Friday
do-yōbi	Saturday
nan-yōbi	what day

date					
month -gatsu		**day** -nichi			
1	ichi-gatsu	1	tsuitachi	17	jū shichi-nichi
2	ni-gatsu	2	futsuka	18	jū hachi-nichi
3	san-gatsu	3	mikka	19	jū ku-nichi
4	shi-gatsu	4	yokka	20	hatsuka
5	go-gatsu	5	itsuka	21	ni-jū ichi-nichi
6	roku-gatsu	6	muika	22	ni-jū ni-nichi
7	shichi-gatsu	7	nanoka	23	ni-jū san-nichi
8	hachi-gatsu	8	yōka	24	ni-jū yokka
9	ku-gatsu	9	kokonoka	25	ni-jū go-nichi
10	jū-gatsu	10	tōka	26	ni-jū roku-nichi
11	jū ichi-gatsu	11	jū ichi-nichi	27	ni-jū shichi-nichi
12	jū ni-gatsu	12	jū ni-nichi	28	ni-jū hachi-nichi
?	nan-gatsu	13	jū san-nichi	29	ni-jū ku-nichi
		14	jū yokka	30	san-jū-nichi
		15	jū go-nichi	31	san-jū ichi-nichi
		16	jū roku-nichi	?	nan-nichi

III. Expressions of period

time duration		
hour -jikan		**minute** -fun/-pun
1	ichi-jikan	ip-pun
2	ni-jikan	ni-fun
3	san-jikan	san-pun
4	yo-jikan	yon-pun
5	go-jikan	go-fun
6	roku-jikan	rop-pun
7	nana-jikan, shichi-jikan	nana-fun
8	hachi-jikan	hap-pun
9	ku-jikan	kyū-fun
10	jū-jikan	jup-pun, jip-pun
?	nan-jikan	nan-pun

period				
	day -nichi	**week** -shūkan	**month** -kagetsu	**year** -nen
1	ichi-nichi	is-shūkan	ik-kagetsu	ichi-nen
2	futsuka	ni-shūkan	ni-kagetsu	ni-nen
3	mikka	san-shūkan	san-kagetsu	san-nen
4	yokka	yon-shūkan	yon-kagetsu	yo-nen
5	itsuka	go-shūkan	go-kagetsu	go-nen
6	muika	roku-shūkan	rok-kagetsu, hantoshi	roku-nen
7	nanoka	nana-shūkan	nana-kagetsu	nana-nen, shichi-nen
8	yōka	has-shūkan	hachi-kagetsu, hak-kagetsu	hachi-nen
9	kokonoka	kyū-shūkan	kyū-kagetsu	kyū-nen
10	tōka	jus-shūkan, jis-shūkan	juk-kagetsu, jik-kagetsu	jū-nen
?	nan-nichi	nan-shūkan	nan-kagetsu	nan-nen

IV. Counter suffixes

	things	persons -nin	order -ban	thin and flat things -mai
1	hitotsu	hitori	ichi-ban	ichi-mai
2	futatsu	futari	ni-ban	ni-mai
3	mittsu	san-nin	san-ban	san-mai
4	yottsu	yo-nin	yon-ban	yon-mai
5	itsutsu	go-nin	go-ban	go-mai
6	muttsu	roku-nin	roku-ban	roku-mai
7	nanatsu	nana-nin, shichi-nin	nana-ban	nana-mai
8	yattsu	hachi-nin	hachi-ban	hachi-mai
9	kokonotsu	kyū-nin	kyū-ban	kyū-mai
10	tō	jū-nin	jū-ban	jū-mai
?	ikutsu	nan-nin	nan-ban	nan-mai

	machines and vehicles -dai	age -sai	books and notebooks -satsu	clothes -chaku
1	ichi-dai	is-sai	is-satsu	it-chaku
2	ni-dai	ni-sai	ni-satsu	ni-chaku
3	san-dai	san-sai	san-satsu	san-chaku
4	yon-dai	yon-sai	yon-satsu	yon-chaku
5	go-dai	go-sai	go-satsu	go-chaku
6	roku-dai	roku-sai	roku-satsu	roku-chaku
7	nana-dai	nana-sai	nana-satsu	nana-chaku
8	hachi-dai	has-sai	has-satsu	hat-chaku
9	kyū-dai	kyū-sai	kyū-satsu	kyū-chaku
10	jū-dai	jus-sai, jis-sai	jus-satsu, jis-satsu	jut-chaku, jit-chaku
?	nan-dai	nan-sai	nan-satsu	nan-chaku

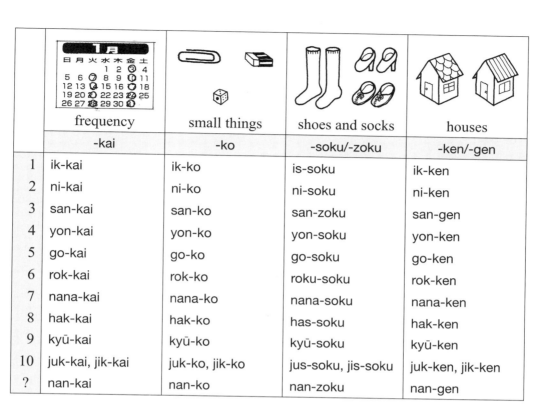

	frequency	small things	shoes and socks	houses
	-kai	-ko	-soku/-zoku	-ken/-gen
1	ik-kai	ik-ko	is-soku	ik-ken
2	ni-kai	ni-ko	ni-soku	ni-ken
3	san-kai	san-ko	san-zoku	san-gen
4	yon-kai	yon-ko	yon-soku	yon-ken
5	go-kai	go-ko	go-soku	go-ken
6	rok-kai	rok-ko	roku-soku	rok-ken
7	nana-kai	nana-ko	nana-soku	nana-ken
8	hak-kai	hak-ko	has-soku	hak-ken
9	kyū-kai	kyū-ko	kyū-soku	kyū-ken
10	juk-kai, jik-kai	juk-ko, jik-ko	jus-soku, jis-soku	juk-ken, jik-ken
?	nan-kai	nan-ko	nan-zoku	nan-gen

169

	floors of a building	thin and long things	drinks, etc., in cups and glasses	small animals, fish and insects
	-kai/-gai	-hon/-pon/-bon	-hai/-pai/-bai	-hiki/-piki/-biki
1	ik-kai	ip-pon	ip-pai	ip-piki
2	ni-kai	ni-hon	ni-hai	ni-hiki
3	san-gai	san-bon	san-bai	san-biki
4	yon-kai	yon-hon	yon-hai	yon-hiki
5	go-kai	go-hon	go-hai	go-hiki
6	rok-kai	rop-pon	rop-pai	rop-piki
7	nana-kai	nana-hon	nana-hai	nana-hiki
8	hak-kai	hap-pon	hap-pai	hap-piki
9	kyū-kai	kyū-hon	kyū-hai	kyū-hiki
10	juk-kai, jik-kai	jup-pon, jip-pon	jup-pai, jip-pai	jup-piki, jip-piki
?	nan-gai	nan-bon	nan-bai	nan-biki

Ⅴ. Conjugations of verbs

Ⅰ - group

	masu-form		te-form	dictionary form
aimasu [tomodachi ni 〜]	ai	masu	atte	au
araimasu	arai	masu	aratte	arau
arimasu	ari	masu	atte	aru
arimasu	ari	masu	atte	aru
arimasu [o-matsuri ga 〜]	ari	masu	atte	aru
arukimasu	aruki	masu	aruite	aruku
asobimasu	asobi	masu	asonde	asobu
dashimasu	dashi	masu	dashite	dasu
furimasu [ame ga 〜]	furi	masu	futte	furu
ganbarimasu	ganbari	masu	ganbatte	ganbaru
hairimasu [daigaku ni 〜]	hairi	masu	haitte	hairu
hairimasu [kissaten ni 〜]	hairi	masu	haitte	hairu
hairimasu [o-furo ni 〜]	hairi	masu	haitte	hairu
hakimasu	haki	masu	haite	haku
hanashimasu	hanashi	masu	hanashite	hanasu
haraimasu	harai	masu	haratte	harau
hatarakimasu	hataraki	masu	hataraite	hataraku
hikimasu	hiki	masu	hiite	hiku
hikimasu	hiki	masu	hiite	hiku
iimasu	ii	masu	itte	iu
ikimasu	iki	masu	itte	iku
irimasu [biza ga 〜]	iri	masu	itte	iru
isogimasu	isogi	masu	isoide	isogu
kaburimasu	kaburi	masu	kabutte	kaburu
kachimasu	kachi	masu	katte	katsu
kaerimasu	kaeri	masu	kaette	kaeru
kaeshimasu	kaeshi	masu	kaeshite	kaesu
kaimasu	kai	masu	katte	kau
kakarimasu	kakari	masu	kakatte	kakaru
kakimasu	kaki	masu	kaite	kaku
kashimasu	kashi	masu	kashite	kasu
keshimasu	keshi	masu	keshite	kesu

nai-form		ta-form	meaning	lesson
awa	nai	atta	meet [a friend]	6
arawa	nai	aratta	wash	18
—	nai	atta	have	9
—	nai	atta	exist, be (referring to inanimate things)	10
—	nai	atta	[a festival] be held, take place	21
aruka	nai	aruita	walk	23
asoba	nai	asonda	enjoy oneself, play	13
dasa	nai	dashita	take out, hand in, send	16
fura	nai	futta	rain	14
ganbara	nai	ganbatta	do one's best	25
haira	nai	haitta	enter [university]	16
haira	nai	haitta	enter [a café]	14
haira	nai	haitta	take [a bath]	17
haka	nai	haita	put on (shoes, trousers, etc.)	22
hanasa	nai	hanashita	speak, talk	14
harawa	nai	haratta	pay	17
hataraka	nai	hataraita	work	4
hika	nai	hiita	play (stringed instrument, piano, etc.)	18
hika	nai	hiita	pull	23
iwa	nai	itta	say	21
ika	nai	itta	go	5
ira	nai	itta	need, require [a visa]	20
isoga	nai	isoida	hurry	14
kabura	nai	kabutta	put on (a hat, etc.)	22
kata	nai	katta	win	21
kaera	nai	kaetta	go home, return	5
kaesa	nai	kaeshita	give back, return	17
kawa	nai	katta	buy	6
kakara	nai	kakatta	take, cost (referring to time or money)	11
kaka	nai	kaita	write, draw, paint	6
kasa	nai	kashita	lend	7
kesa	nai	keshita	turn off	14

171

	masu-form		te-form	dictionary form
kikimasu	kiki	masu	kiite	kiku
kikimasu [sensei ni ～]	kiki	masu	kiite	kiku
kirimasu	kiri	masu	kitte	kiru
machimasu	machi	masu	matte	matsu
magarimasu [migi e ～]	magari	masu	magatte	magaru
mawashimasu	mawashi	masu	mawashite	mawasu
mochimasu	mochi	masu	motte	motsu
moraimasu	morai	masu	moratte	morau
motte ikimasu	motte iki	masu	motte itte	motte iku
nakushimasu	nakushi	masu	nakushite	nakusu
naoshimasu	naoshi	masu	naoshite	naosu
naraimasu	narai	masu	naratte	narau
narimasu	nari	masu	natte	naru
noborimasu	nobori	masu	nobotte	noboru
nomimasu	nomi	masu	nonde	nomu
nomimasu	nomi	masu	nonde	nomu
nomimasu [kusuri o ～]	nomi	masu	nonde	nomu
norimasu [densha ni ～]	nori	masu	notte	noru
nugimasu	nugi	masu	nuide	nugu
okimasu	oki	masu	oite	oku
okurimasu	okuri	masu	okutte	okuru
okurimasu [hito o ～]	okuri	masu	okutte	okuru
omoidashimasu	omoidashi	masu	omoidashite	omoidasu
omoimasu	omoi	masu	omotte	omou
oroshimasu [okane o ～]	oroshi	masu	oroshite	orosu
oshimasu	oshi	masu	oshite	osu
owarimasu	owari	masu	owatte	owaru
oyogimasu	oyogi	masu	oyoide	oyogu
sawarimasu [doa ni ～]	sawari	masu	sawatte	sawaru
shirimasu	shiri	masu	shitte	shiru
suimasu [tabako o ～]	sui	masu	sutte	suu
sumimasu	sumi	masu	sunde	sumu
suwarimasu	suwari	masu	suwatte	suwaru
tachimasu	tachi	masu	tatte	tatsu

nai-form		ta-form	meaning	lesson
kika	nai	kiita	hear, listen	6
kika	nai	kiita	ask [the teacher]	23
kira	nai	kitta	cut, slice	7
mata	nai	matta	wait	14
magara	nai	magatta	turn [to the right]	23
mawasa	nai	mawashita	turn	23
mota	nai	motta	hold	14
morawa	nai	moratta	receive	7
motte ika	nai	motte itta	take (something)	17
nakusa	nai	nakushita	lose	17
naosa	nai	naoshita	repair, correct	24
narawa	nai	naratta	learn	7
nara	nai	natta	become	19
nobora	nai	nobotta	climb, go up	19
noma	nai	nonda	drink	6
noma	nai	nonda	drink alcohol	16
noma	nai	nonda	take [medicine]	17
nora	nai	notta	ride, get on [a train]	16
nuga	nai	nuida	take off (clothes, shoes, etc.)	17
oka	nai	oita	put	15
okura	nai	okutta	send	7
okura	nai	okutta	escort [someone], go with	24
omoidasa	nai	omoidashita	remember, recollect	15
omowa	nai	omotta	think	21
orosa	nai	oroshita	withdraw	16
osa	nai	oshita	push, press	16
owara	nai	owatta	finish	4
oyoga	nai	oyoida	swim	13
sawara	nai	sawatta	touch [a door]	23
shira	nai	shitta	get to know	15
suwa	nai	sutta	smoke [a cigarette]	6
suma	nai	sunda	be going to live	15
suwara	nai	suwatta	sit down	14
tata	nai	tatta	stand up	14

	masu-form		te-form	dictionary form
tetsudaimasu	tetsudai	masu	tetsudatte	tetsudau
tomarimasu [hoteru ni ～]	tomari	masu	tomatte	tomaru
torimasu	tori	masu	totte	toru
torimasu [shashin o ～]	tori	masu	totte	toru
torimasu [toshi o ～]	tori	masu	totte	toru
tsukaimasu	tsukai	masu	tsukatte	tsukau
tsukimasu	tsuki	masu	tsuite	tsuku
tsukurimasu	tsukuri	masu	tsukutte	tsukuru
tsurete ikimasu	tsurete iki	masu	tsurete itte	tsurete iku
ugokimasu	ugoki	masu	ugoite	ugoku
urimasu	uri	masu	utte	uru
utaimasu	utai	masu	utatte	utau
wakarimasu	wakari	masu	wakatte	wakaru
watarimasu [hashi o ～]	watari	masu	watatte	wataru
yaku ni tachimasu	yaku ni tachi	masu	yaku ni tatte	yaku ni tatsu
yasumimasu	yasumi	masu	yasunde	yasumu
yasumimasu [kaisha o ～]	yasumi	masu	yasunde	yasumu
yobimasu	yobi	masu	yonde	yobu
yomimasu	yomi	masu	yonde	yomu

nai-form		ta-form	meaning	lesson
tetsudawa	nai	tetsudatta	help (with a task)	14
tomara	nai	tomatta	stay [at a hotel]	19
tora	nai	totta	take, pass	14
tora	nai	totta	take [a photograph]	6
tora	nai	totta	grow old	25
tsukawa	nai	tsukatta	use	14
tsuka	nai	tsuita	arrive	25
tsukura	nai	tsukutta	make, produce	15
tsurete ika	nai	tsurete itta	take (someone)	24
ugoka	nai	ugoita	move, work	21
ura	nai	utta	sell	15
utawa	nai	utatta	sing	18
wakara	nai	wakatta	understand	9
watara	nai	watatta	cross [a bridge]	23
yaku ni tata	nai	yaku ni tatta	be useful	21
yasuma	nai	yasunda	take a rest, take a holiday	4
yasuma	nai	yasunda	take a day off [work]	11
yoba	nai	yonda	call	14
yoma	nai	yonda	read	6

II – group

	masu-form		te-form	dictionary form
abimasu [shawā o 〜]	abi	masu	abite	abiru
agemasu	age	masu	agete	ageru
akemasu	ake	masu	akete	akeru
atsumemasu	atsume	masu	atsumete	atsumeru
dekakemasu	dekake	masu	dekakete	dekakeru
dekimasu	deki	masu	dekite	dekiru
demasu [daigaku o 〜]	de	masu	dete	deru
demasu [kissaten o 〜]	de	masu	dete	deru
demasu [otsuri ga 〜]	de	masu	dete	deru
hajimemasu	hajime	masu	hajimete	hajimeru
imasu	i	masu	ite	iru
imasu [kodomo ga 〜]	i	masu	ite	iru
imasu [Nihon ni 〜]	i	masu	ite	iru
iremasu	ire	masu	irete	ireru
kaemasu	kae	masu	kaete	kaeru
kaemasu	kae	masu	kaete	kaeru
kakemasu [denwa o 〜]	kake	masu	kakete	kakeru
kakemasu [megane o 〜]	kake	masu	kakete	kakeru
kangaemasu	kangae	masu	kangaete	kangaeru
karimasu	kari	masu	karite	kariru
kimasu	ki	masu	kite	kiru
ki o tsukemasu	ki o tsuke	masu	ki o tsukete	ki o tsukeru
kuremasu	kure	masu	kurete	kureru
makemasu	make	masu	makete	makeru
mimasu	mi	masu	mite	miru
misemasu	mise	masu	misete	miseru
mukaemasu	mukae	masu	mukaete	mukaeru
nemasu	ne	masu	nete	neru
norikaemasu	norikae	masu	norikaete	norikaeru
oboemasu	oboe	masu	oboete	oboeru
okimasu	oki	masu	okite	okiru
orimasu [densha o 〜]	ori	masu	orite	oriru
oshiemasu	oshie	masu	oshiete	oshieru

nai-form		ta-form	meaning	lesson
abi	nai	abita	take [a shower]	16
age	nai	ageta	give	7
ake	nai	aketa	open	14
atsume	nai	atsumeta	collect, gather	18
dekake	nai	dekaketa	go out	17
deki	nai	dekita	be able to, can	18
de	nai	deta	graduate from [university]	16
de	nai	deta	go out [of a café]	14
de	nai	deta	[change] come out	23
hajime	nai	hajimeta	start, begin	16
i	nai	ita	exist, be (referring to animate things)	10
i	nai	ita	have [a child]	11
i	nai	ita	stay, be [in Japan]	11
ire	nai	ireta	put in, insert	16
kae	nai	kaeta	exchange, change	18
kae	nai	kaeta	change	23
kake	nai	kaketa	make [a telephone call]	7
kake	nai	kaketa	put on [glasses]	22
kangae	nai	kangaeta	think, consider	25
kari	nai	karita	borrow	7
ki	nai	kita	put on (a shirt, etc.)	22
ki o tsuke	nai	ki o tsuketa	pay attention, take care	21
kure	nai	kureta	give (me)	24
make	nai	maketa	lose, be beaten	21
mi	nai	mita	see, look at, watch	6
mise	nai	miseta	show	14
mukae	nai	mukaeta	go to meet, welcome	13
ne	nai	neta	sleep, go to bed	4
norikae	nai	norikaeta	change (train, etc.)	16
oboe	nai	oboeta	memorise	17
oki	nai	okita	get up, wake up	4
ori	nai	orita	get off [a train]	16
oshie	nai	oshieta	teach	7

	masu-form		te-form	dictionary form
oshiemasu [jūsho o 〜]	oshie	masu	oshiete	oshieru
shimemasu	shime	masu	shimete	shimeru
shirabemasu	shirabe	masu	shirabete	shiraberu
sutemasu	sute	masu	sutete	suteru
tabemasu	tabe	masu	tabete	taberu
tarimasu	tari	masu	tarite	tariru
tomemasu	tome	masu	tomete	tomeru
tsukaremasu	tsukare	masu	tsukarete	tsukareru
tsukemasu	tsuke	masu	tsukete	tsukeru
umaremasu	umare	masu	umarete	umareru
wasuremasu	wasure	masu	wasurete	wasureru
yamemasu [kaisha o 〜]	yame	masu	yamete	yameru

nai-form		ta-form	meaning	lesson
oshie	nai	oshieta	tell [an address]	14
shime	nai	shimeta	close, shut	14
shirabe	nai	shirabeta	check, investigate	20
sute	nai	suteta	throw away	18
tabe	nai	tabeta	eat	6
tari	nai	tarita	be enough, be sufficient	25
tome	nai	tometa	stop, park	14
tsukare	nai	tsukareta	get tired	13
tsuke	nai	tsuketa	turn on	14
umare	nai	umareta	be born	22
wasure	nai	wasureta	forget	17
yame	nai	yameta	quit or retire from [a company], stop, give up	21

III – group

	masu-form		te-form	dictionary form
annai-shimasu	annai-shi	masu	annai-shite	annai-suru
benkyō-shimasu	benkyō-shi	masu	benkyō-shite	benkyō-suru
denwa-shimasu	denwa-shi	masu	denwa-shite	denwa-suru
kaimono-shimasu	kaimono-shi	masu	kaimono-shite	kaimono-suru
kekkon-shimasu	kekkon-shi	masu	kekkon-shite	kekkon-suru
kengaku-shimasu	kengaku-shi	masu	kengaku-shite	kengaku-suru
kenkyū-shimasu	kenkyū-shi	masu	kenkyū-shite	kenkyū-suru
kimasu	ki	masu	kite	kuru
kopii-shimasu	kopii-shi	masu	kopii-shite	kopii-suru
motte kimasu	motte ki	masu	motte kite	motte kuru
ryūgaku-shimasu	ryūgaku-shi	masu	ryūgaku-shite	ryūgaku-suru
sanpo-shimasu [kōen o ～]	sanpo-shi	masu	sanpo-shite	sanpo-suru
sentaku-shimasu	sentaku-shi	masu	sentaku-shite	sentaku-suru
setsumei-shimasu	setsumei-shi	masu	setsumei-shite	setsumei-suru
shimasu	shi	masu	shite	suru
shimasu [nekutai o ～]	shi	masu	shite	suru
shinpai-shimasu	shinpai-shi	masu	shinpai-shite	shinpai-suru
shōkai-shimasu	shōkai-shi	masu	shōkai-shite	shōkai-suru
shokuji-shimasu	shokuji-shi	masu	shokuji-shite	shokuji-suru
shūri-shimasu	shūri-shi	masu	shūri-shite	shūri-suru
shutchō-shimasu	shutchō-shi	masu	shutchō-shite	shutchō-suru
sōji-shimasu	sōji-shi	masu	sōji-shite	sōji-suru
tsurete kimasu	tsurete ki	masu	tsurete kite	tsurete kuru
unten-shimasu	unten-shi	masu	unten-shite	unten-suru
yoyaku-shimasu	yoyaku-shi	masu	yoyaku-shite	yoyaku-suru
zangyō-shimasu	zangyō-shi	masu	zangyō-shite	zangyō-suru

nai-form		ta-form	meaning	lesson
annai-shi	nai	annai-shita	show around, show the way	24
benkyō-shi	nai	benkyō-shita	study	4
denwa-shi	nai	denwa-shita	phone	16
kaimono-shi	nai	kaimono-shita	do shopping	13
kekkon-shi	nai	kekkon-shita	marry, get married	13
kengaku-shi	nai	kengaku-shita	tour, visit a place to study it	16
kenkyū-shi	nai	kenkyū-shita	do research	15
ko	nai	kita	come	5
kopii-shi	nai	kopii-shita	copy	14
motte ko	nai	motte kita	bring (something)	17
ryūgaku-shi	nai	ryūgaku-shita	study abroad	21
sanpo-shi	nai	sanpo-shita	take a walk [in a park]	13
sentaku-shi	nai	sentaku-shita	wash (clothes)	19
setsumei-shi	nai	setsumei-shita	explain	24
shi	nai	shita	do, play	6
shi	nai	shita	put on [tie]	22
shinpai-shi	nai	shinpai-shita	worry	17
shōkai-shi	nai	shōkai-shita	introduce	24
shokuji-shi	nai	shokuji-shita	have a meal, dine	13
shūri-shi	nai	shūri-shita	repair	20
shutchō-shi	nai	shutchō-shita	go on a business trip	17
sōji-shi	nai	sōji-shita	clean (a room)	19
tsurete ko	nai	tsurete kita	bring (someone)	24
unten-shi	nai	unten-shita	drive	18
yoyaku-shi	nai	yoyaku-shita	reserve, book	18
zangyō-shi	nai	zangyō-shita	work overtime	17

監修　Supervisors
鶴尾能子（Tsuruo Yoshiko）　石沢弘子（Ishizawa Hiroko）

執筆協力　Contributors
田中よね（Tanaka Yone）　澤田幸子（Sawada Sachiko）　重川明美（Shigekawa Akemi）
牧野昭子（Makino Akiko）　御子神慶子（Mikogami Keiko）

英語翻訳　English translator
John H. Loftus

本文イラスト　Illustrators
田辺澄美（Tanabe Kiyomi）　佐藤夏枝（Sato Natsue）

装丁・本文デザイン　Cover and Layout Designer
山田武（Yamada Takeshi）

写真提供
栃木県、姫路市、広島県

みんなの日本語 初級I 第2版
翻訳・文法解説　ローマ字版【英語】

2000年10月20日　初版第1刷発行
2013年 2月20日　第2版第1刷発行
2019年 2月22日　第2版第7刷発行

編著者　　スリーエーネットワーク
発行者　　藤嵜政子
発　行　　株式会社スリーエーネットワーク
　　　　　〒102-0083　東京都千代田区麹町3丁目4番
　　　　　　　　　　　トラスティ麹町ビル2F
　　　　　電話　営業　03(5275)2722
　　　　　　　　編集　03(5275)2725
　　　　　http://www.3anet.co.jp/
印　刷　　倉敷印刷株式会社

ISBN978-4-88319-629-6 C0081

みんなの日本語シリーズ

みんなの日本語 初級I 第2版

● 本冊(CD付) ················· 2,500円+税
● 本冊 ローマ字版(CD付) ···· 2,500円+税
● 翻訳・文法解説 ········· 各2,000円+税
英語版／ローマ字版【英語】／中国語版／
韓国語版／ドイツ語版／スペイン語版／ポ
ルトガル語版／ベトナム語版／イタリア語
版／フランス語版／ロシア語版(新版)／タ
イ語版／インドネシア語版／ビルマ語版
● 教え方の手引き ············· 2,800円+税
● 初級で読めるトピック25 ···· 1,400円+税
● 聴解タスク25 ················· 2,000円+税
● 標準問題集 ··················· 900円+税
● 漢字 英語版 ················· 1,800円+税
● 漢字 ベトナム語版 ··········· 1,800円+税
● 漢字練習帳 ··················· 900円+税
● 書いて覚える文型練習帳 ····· 1,300円+税
● 導入・練習イラスト集 ········· 2,200円+税
● CD 5枚セット ··············· 8,000円+税
● 会話DVD ··················· 8,000円+税
● 会話DVD　PAL方式 ········ 8,000円+税
● 絵教材CD-ROMブック ······· 3,000円+税

みんなの日本語 初級II 第2版

● 本冊(CD付) ················· 2,500円+税
● 翻訳・文法解説 ··········· 各2,000円+税
英語版／中国語版／韓国語版／ドイツ語
版／スペイン語版／ポルトガル語版／ベ
トナム語版／イタリア語版／フランス語
版／ロシア語版(新版)／タイ語版／イン
ドネシア語版

みんなの日本語 初級 第2版

● やさしい作文 ················· 1,200円+税

みんなの日本語 中級I

● 本冊(CD付) ················· 2,800円+税
● 翻訳・文法解説 ············· 各1,600円+税
英語版／中国語版／韓国語版／ドイツ語
版／スペイン語版／ポルトガル語版／フ
ランス語版／ベトナム語版
● 教え方の手引き ············· 2,500円+税
● 標準問題集 ··················· 900円+税
● くり返して覚える単語帳 ········ 900円+税

みんなの日本語 中級II

● 本冊(CD付) ················· 2,800円+税
● 翻訳・文法解説 ············· 各1,800円+税
英語版／中国語版／韓国語版／ドイツ語
版／スペイン語版／ポルトガル語版／フ
ランス語版／ベトナム語版
● 教え方の手引き ············· 2,500円+税
● 標準問題集 ··················· 900円+税
● くり返して覚える単語帳 ········ 900円+税

右列上部：
● 教え方の手引き ············· 2,800円+税
● 初級で読めるトピック25 ···· 1,400円+税
● 聴解タスク25 ················· 2,400円+税
● 標準問題集 ··················· 900円+税
● 漢字 英語版 ················· 1,800円+税
● 漢字練習帳 ················· 1,200円+税
● 書いて覚える文型練習帳 ····· 1,300円+税
● 導入・練習イラスト集 ········· 2,400円+税
● CD 5枚セット ··············· 8,000円+税
● 会話DVD ··················· 8,000円+税
● 会話DVD　PAL方式 ········ 8,000円+税
● 絵教材CD-ROMブック ······· 3,000円+税

● 小説 ミラーさん
　　―みんなの日本語初級シリーズ―
　　······················· 1,000円+税

スリーエーネットワーク

ウェブサイトで新刊や日本語セミナーをご案内しております。
http://www.3anet.co.jp/